SECRETS OF LEADERSHIP MASTERY

22 POWERFUL KEYS TO UNLOCK YOUR TEAM'S POTENTIAL AND GET GREATER RESULTS

Mike Agugliaro

ISBN-13: 978-1512066241
ISBN-10: 1512066249

CONTENTS

INTRODUCTION

Think back to when you first started in your business: you probably had a manager or supervisor who helped you as you worked through your apprenticeship and earned your certifications or licenses. Chances are, you motivated yourself to learn because you wanted a career and you wanted to earn the kind of money that seemed possible as a business owner, instead of working for someone else. And, you were probably also motivated by your manager or supervisor to follow their rules, show up on time, and complete your work with excellence.

Fast forward to today. You've been in your service business for a while and now you find yourself as a manager – perhaps you oversee a team for a company or perhaps you own the company. The tables have turned: once, you worked for someone else and did what they told you; now you are leading a team and asking them to follow your lead.

Leadership is one of the hardest skills to learn. Unlike other skills where each of the building blocks is finite and unchanging, leadership is a highly challenging skill because you're leading people – imperfect people with their own targets and desires and motivations (and problems and quirks). And you're not just leading one person but multiple people, which compounds the challenge.

Leadership is also an opportunity: it's an opportunity to inspire a group of diverse people (each with their own targets and desires and motivations) to work together collaboratively, to follow your example and perform their work to the level of excellence that you establish. When you lead a group like this, you create a strong business that has the potential to succeed and grow, and even to run without you.

On the following pages I'll show you 22 powerful keys of leadership mastery that can transform your business. These same keys helped me to lead my team as it grew to an over-$23 million dollar business with over 140 employees.

In each chapter I have included Take Action sections where I encourage you to pause in your reading and actually turn your reading into action. Each Take Action section contains space for you to add specific actions you'll take as a result of the lessons you've learned: there are areas to write **actions you will stop doing** (actions you currently do but need to cease), **actions you will keep doing** (actions you currently do now and should continue), and **actions you will start doing** (actions you don't do now but should begin). I've also included space for you to make a note about **when you'll make these changes** and **who you might help you do them** (for example, you might delegate to an employee or you might ask someone to hold you accountable to complete the step).

There's something you should know first: these 22 powerful keys of leadership mastery are extremely effective but only if you first make sure that they are built on a strong foundation. That strong foundation starts with solid core values, good hiring practices, a good reputation in the industry (among peers and customers). In my book *The Secrets Of Business Mastery*, I explain how to master 12 key areas of your business that will transform how you run your business and give you the foundation to build on. This book can be read on its own or in conjunction with *The Secrets Of Business Mastery*.

POWER KEY #1: THE WAY YOU'VE BEEN THINKING ABOUT YOUR EMPLOYEES IS NUTS

Your employees are the biggest assets you have. Their performance and attitude can make or break your business. But many business owners find the leap from being the technician (who does the work) to being the boss/owner/leader (who directs others to do the work) is one of the most difficult leaps you can make. Those are very different responsibilities so it's no surprise that many business owners struggle to lead a team.

Leadership encompasses the tasks of:

- Finding the right people and keeping them (and sometimes letting the wrong people go).
- Inspiring them to work for you and to give you their best every day.
- Ensuring that they have the strategies and skills to do their job.
- Ensuring that administrative work (including benefits and salary) are up to date... *remember, you get what you pay for.*

You may not do all of these things yourself but as the one in charge, you need to make sure these are done. Some days, it may not seem easy to do. How do you find the right people? How do you inspire them to work? How do you juggle all the training and administrative work?

Let's start with you. In this book I'll describe many strategies you can implement in your business to help you lead the people in your business but before you implement any other changes that you read about here, you need to first start with yourself and change how you've been thinking.

Chances are, you see your job as a wrangler – like an Old West cowboy who had to corral wild horses – perhaps you see yourself as someone who needs to corral a whole bunch of staff who don't want to be there and who just want to earn a paycheck and go home. I meet a lot of business owners who feel this way about their team.

But here's why that's nuts: With the right person in charge, a good team will follow well, they'll do an excellent job, and they'll help you grow your business. So rather than cajoling and threatening and begging them to do their work (which is what a wrangler would do), **lead** them. Stop being a wrangler. You will instantly discover more effective management – and results from your team – when you lead. Take charge of your team.

The shift from reluctant wrangler to inspiring leader is a total change of mindset for you and it will be a massive shift for your company.

You will see dramatic improvements in the people who join your team and you'll see dramatic improvements in how your team works. And when this happens, you'll discover that you'll have more time to devote to other things – such as working on your business instead of in your business, and even more free time than you had before!

It doesn't work to just hope for improvement. You need to make sure you can see in your own mind the leader you want to be. Do this by identifying on paper the values you will personally lead by. For example, here are some values to lead by:

- A leader is clear and direct – he knows what he wants and he explains it to his team in a way that leaves no room for doubt what his expectations are.
- A leader is fearless – willing to do the hard work of finding the right people for their business and even cutting the wrong people.
- A leader is inspiring and motivating – his employees see him as someone who will help them achieve their goals.
- A leader is positive – someone who elevates his team daily so they want to give their best.

The simplest way to start achieving this type of leadership is by discovering what motivates your team members. Each of your team members are thinking, feeling individuals, just like you. They have goals in life; they have something that motivates them to show up to work. They have a "why" that they will work hard for. It might be that they want to send their child to college, or they want to support a hobby like restoring a class car, or maybe they want the opportunity to learn so they can run their own business someday.

When you discover the "why" of each of your team members, you can inspire them to give their very best to you so you can help them enjoy or fulfill their "why."

As you'll discover with all of my thinking and writing about running a business, it all comes back to serving. Just as you and your employees serve your customers, you serve your employees. Serve your employees and they'll work hard for you.

This "why" discovery and this idea of serving will change everything: it helps you find and recruit the best team members, it helps you motivate and inspire your team, and it will even help you let someone go from your company.

I love this approach to running a business. When you step up as a leader, you build a team who gives their very best because they achieve their own goals. And when your team gives their very best, your customers are served. And when your customers are served, your business grows. Everyone wins.

So before we continue, commit to yourself to stop being a manager or a wrangler or a reluctant boss. Be a leader.

Take Action!

(Add a checkmark beside each one when complete):

__ Stop doing actions (Actions you currently do now but should stop doing)

_____

_____

__ Keep doing actions (Actions you currently do now and should keep doing)

_____

_____

__ Start doing actions (Actions you don't do now but should start doing)

_____

_____

__ Who will do new actions? (Assign the action to yourself or someone else)

_____

_____

__ By when? (When will these actions be complete?)

_____

_____

POWER KEY #2: HOW A FEW SMALL WORDS CAN MAKE OR BREAK YOUR SUCCESS

For a ship captain in charge of a boat that is propelled by rowers, leading and motivating the individuals responsible for rowing is necessary, and it is equally important to steer the ship in the right direction. However, the best navigation in the world makes no difference if the oarsmen are rowing in opposite directions. Like a ship captain, you as a leader must first focus everyone's energy in the same direction.

This can be particularly challenging because your team does not have the same perspective as you. In the analogy above, the oarsmen are below deck and they are focused on just one thing: moving their oar back and forth. They can't see where the ship is headed – that's the captain's job. Likewise, your team is busy serving customers one at a time, fixing furnaces or leaky faucets or broken outlets. They're focused on today; they don't your perspective as the business owner.

So how do you communicate that purpose? Leadership is about much more than simply conveying your destination or your vision. It also means you, as a leader, must take steps to motivate and direct everyone to focus their energy on reaching that destination. You do this by inspiring and motivating them, training and coaching them, and making sure that all team members are fully equipped with everything they need to do their job with an understanding of how it all fits together.

Start with a core purpose for your business. A core purpose is the reason why you are in business.

Create your core purpose for your business (or if you already have one, consider updating it). Gather these elements together:

- List all the details of your business – who, what, where, when, and how of your business.
- Determine what you want to deliver to your customers – the high level commitment you make as a business that serves them.
- Identify the "why" of your business – what motivates you and your team to serve others?
- Describe what you hope to achieve in your business – for the business itself, for yourself, for your employees, and for your customers.
- Describe what makes you unique – why customers might call you instead of anyone else.

- Think beyond the basics like profit or size. Think big. Think of the impact you can have in your city, state, or even the world. Find something that will truly inspire you (and your team).

Tie these pieces together into a succinct statement of just one or two sentences that expresses the reason you're in business. Here are some examples that might help you…

Here's my own core purpose to give you another example and to show you how high I'm reaching in my business:

- To create a movement and change the life of every service business owner so they can have more wealth, freedom, time with their family, and be appreciated in an industry that makes a difference in our comfort and safety and in how we live.

Now double-check your core purpose against what you actually do. Are all of your company's products/services in line with your core purpose? Are all of your employees in line with your core purpose? Are all of your team's daily activities in line with your core purpose? Are all of YOUR daily activities in line with your core purpose?

Then have employees, customers, associates, and even strangers read your core purpose and interpret it to you. Does it say what you want it to say? Your core purpose has to be perfectly clear. Anyone should be able to instantly understand what you promise others.

Your core purpose helps you to succinctly communicate to your team the direction you want your business to go. And it helps to share your perspective with your team so they can all row the boat in the same direction. When you embed your business' core purpose into your employees' minds, it becomes a filter to help them know what to do and say in almost every situation, and a way to help them make decisions when you're not around to give them advice.

Now that you've created a core purpose for your business, you can even take it one step further: Have everyone on your team create their own core purpose. All employees – from your executive team to the janitorial staff – should create their own core purposes. These individual core purposes will be unique to them and should take into account their work plus their "why." It should connect what they do for you and the reason they do it.

This action will help your team articulate the reasons why they work (and why they work for you). The result: team members will become more responsible for their work, more proactive, and more productive because they'll have connected the work they do for you with the reason why they need to work. Their core purpose becomes a constant reminder to them of the importance of doing a great job for you.

My individual core purpose in my business is to make every interaction with my customers amazing.

By taking this extra step, you are serving your team by helping them understand and articulate exactly why they show up to work and what they are committing to now and in the future.

You may find that some employees create purpose statements that are focused on helping family members or doing good deeds in the community, while others have high aspirations to grow big businesses themselves. Encourage them to connect those dreams to the work they do today and to articulate in their own personal core purposes how their work will help them achieve their dreams.

By doing this, you'll find that most of your employees will become far more engaged at work and inspired to go the extra mile while serving your customers. And truthfully, you might find that some employees realize they just aren't fulfilling their core purpose in your business or contributing to your business' core purpose and they may choose to leave your company – that's okay because this is a great way to ensure that you build a team of employees who fit.

Take Action!

__ Stop doing actions (Actions you currently do now but should stop doing)

_____

_____

__ Keep doing actions (Actions you currently do now and should keep doing)

_____

_____

__ Start doing actions (Actions you don't do now but should start doing)

_____

_____

__ Who will do new actions? (Assign the action to yourself or someone else)

_____

_____

__ By when? (When will these actions be complete?)

_____

_____

POWER KEY #3: SYSTEMS: THE SECRET INGREDIENT TO FAST TRACK GROWTH

When you started in the business, it was probably just you doing all the work. You knew exactly what needed to happen and you did it. Now that you have employees, your role is changing and you're probably discovering that recruiting, training, motivating, and leading employees can be a lot of work.

As a leader, you can't be everywhere at once. How often do you find yourself answering employee questions during the day? How often do you find yourself solving problems or challenges that your employees are facing? How often do you find yourself guiding your team and pointing them in the right direction?

Leading a team takes a lot of time and work — more than most people have to give. So one of the best things you can do is to create systems and put them in place to help your employees.

Systems are step-by-step directions meant to keep one small part of your business aligned. For example, you might have a system for how to answer the phone, which is a checklist with the words to say when you answer the phone, the questions to ask, the information to take down, and then what to do with the information once the call is done.

Sometimes one system is enough. But sometimes you need to string together several systems in your business to make something work correctly, and I call those "processes." A process is a string of systems that moves something along in a chain, often through multiple departments. A good example would be a money-handling process: You have a system for the employee accepting the check from the customer and giving it to someone in the finance department, a system for the finance department receiving the check and making sure the payment is associated with the correct account owing, and then a system for bringing the check to the bank. These are a few independent systems that work together as a process.

Your business needs both. Start with systems for various parts of your business and then string them together into processes when appropriate.

Systems will automate a lot of your own effort and take it out of your daily schedule. Systems won't replace you or eliminate all of your work but they'll help to reduce the attention you have to give to every single request or challenge that your employees have. Systems will also empower your employees to do their work effectively and consistently (without you feeling like you need to watch over their shoulder). Systems move the pieces forward with consistent results.

Even developing your core purpose in a previous chapter is a type of system – as I mentioned, your core purpose becomes a filter for your employees to know what to do and say when you're not around and it helps them to make decisions that will help the business.

There are many other systems you can put in place – from key employee documents, which I'll talk about in the next chapters, to hiring and training systems, which I'll talk about later in this book.

Systems are essential to being an effective leader and to ensuring that your team is consistently serving your customers to the highest level. Consider McDonald's restaurants – whether or not you like their food, you have to admit that they have become massively successful worldwide even though they are staffed almost entirely by minimum wage teenagers. Their secret? Absolutely everything has a system, from the moment the store opens in the morning to the moment the lights are turned off at night.

Systems aren't only for large companies like McDonald's. Your business will thrive when you put systems in place. They'll give you more time and your employees more direction, and systems will help your business grow.

Which systems should you create? Many of the strategies in this book are systems so you should start with these. But another good rule of thumb is: Whenever you have to do something more than once, even if it's as simple as answering a question more than once, develop a system for it.

Another reason to create a system is to solve a problem. For example, I was being frequently interrupted from my daily work to deal with various situations – some important and some not so important. So I implemented a really simple system to help people quickly tell me the level of importance of their interruption: I call it the "1-3-5 system" and whenever someone reaches out to me during the day through phone, email, or face-to-face, they give me a quick assessment of the level of importance of the conversation: A "1" tells me that someone is just saying hello and wants a friendly non-time-sensitive conversation. A "3" tells me that it's important but it can wait. A "5" tells me that there's an urgent, important customer or money issue that I need to address right away.

Once implemented, this simple system cleared up my schedule and allowed me to focus. And that's exactly what I'm recommending for you when you create systems: develop systems that help your employees know what to do and that free you up to focus on the most important work in your business.

Systems don't completely eliminate all future work for you. You'll need to monitor the system and make sure that it's still working for you and that there haven't been shifts in the market or your business that have made the system less useful. But a system can automate parts of your business so you can turn those systems on, let them run, and focus on other work.

What do I recommend for all business owners? Start thinking about systems and putting them in place. Build systems to lead your team (since this IS a book on leadership) but move beyond that and build systems to run your entire business.

If you want to know more about systems, and create powerful systems and processes for your business, I devote an entire chapter to it in my book *The Secrets Of Business Mastery*. But in this chapter, you have enough to get you started.

Take Action!

__ Stop doing actions (Actions you currently do now but should stop doing)

_____

_____

__ Keep doing actions (Actions you currently do now and should keep doing)

_____

_____

__ Start doing actions (Actions you don't do now but should start doing)

_____

_____

__ Who will do new actions? (Assign the action to yourself or someone else)

_____

_____

___ By when? (When will these actions be complete?)

_____

_____

POWER KEY #4: HOW TO QUICKLY ALIGN YOUR TEAM AND GET EVERYONE MOVING FORWARD

When someone joins your team, they bring their own experiences and ideas and attitudes with them. And, while it's good to have that unique perspective on your team, it's your job as the business owner to ensure that everyone works together for the good of the customer, the good of the team, and the good of the business.

To help your employees get on the same page, an employee handbook helps to spell out the procedures and guidelines that you set in place.

Everyone benefits with an employee handbook: you benefit because you set the procedures and guidelines once and they remain in writing and unchanged; your employees benefit because they get a clear description of exactly what you expect them to do (and not to do); your team as a whole benefits because the handbook helps to clarify expectations and prevent disagreements; your customers benefit because it outlines how you expect your employees to act, look, and talk around customers so customers get consistent, professional service.

Here's how to create your employee handbook:

First, identify the procedures and guidelines you want to include in your handbook. To help you ensure that you are creating a comprehensive list, consider a typical day – from when the employee is on their way to work in the morning to when they leave for home at the end of the day. Address how they act, look, talk, and their actions at each step.

At the end of this chapter I've included a comprehensive list of topics that you can use as a starting point.

Once you have a large list, identify ways to measure each piece. That way, you can hold employees accountable to a clear standard that is not open to interpretation.

After completing the first draft of your handbook, be sure to seek legal advice for a review of terminology and wording that best protects you. Courts will often interpret any vague provisions in the favor of employees if any action is brought against you. A written handbook, with clear, legal writing, is your best chance of not having a court case become your word against an employee's word.

To avoid legal pitfalls in the wording of these sections have your lawyer insert a disclaimer. Courts have a record of upholding the "employment-at-will" doctrine in which the company expressly states that employment can be terminated at any time, for any reason. A disclaimer should also appear when there is any mention of firing and disciplinary procedures. Sometimes an immediate firing of an employee is required. To protect against a lawsuit in such a case, a statement such as the following should appear with the list of unacceptable conduct: "This list is intended as an example only and is not intended to include all acts that could lead to employee discipline." With this statement, an employee contesting termination because embezzlement wasn't specifically listed in the handbook will have no grounds.

Be careful not to use restrictive language when you are writing policy. Words such as "will" or "must" might bind you to actions you did not intend. Also avoid any probationary periods of employment. Use words such as "training" or "orientation" for a trial period. When practical, explain the reasons for policies.

I'm listing the things you need in your employee handbook but it shouldn't just be a list of procedures and guidelines with a bunch of legal phrases thrown in. Those are important components but your employee handbook should be encouraging and upbeat and should include some general history about your company and the benefits of employment.

Employee handbook topics:

Be sure to include the pertinent information listed below in your employee handbook, along with any other issues your company needs to address. Also, remain as succinct as possible:

- **Company Overview** – Consider this the introduction to your company. In it, you could include your core values, brand promise, core purpose, history, growth, and targets.
- **Equal Opportunity Statement** – State that an employee's religion, age, sex, or race will have nothing to do with hiring, promotion, pay, or benefits.
- **Work Hours** – Define the normal work week, start time, end time, lunch, and breaks.
- **Pay and Performance** – No specific numbers are needed here. General statements about paydays, pay periods, how promotions and wage increases are handled, classification of employees (part-time, full-time, on-call) and policies on leaves without pay, overtime, and other pay irregularities are sufficient. This is also the area for policy on performance reviews. Employees should know in exactly what areas they will be evaluated and how often. You could also state that written evaluations can occur at any time to advise workers of unsatisfactory performance.

- **Benefits** – Include insurance company brochures that explain your insurance policies. Define who is eligible for insurance, how long a new employee must wait for coverage, and what portion of premium costs the company covers. Include any additional insurance options such as dental or disability that employees can buy through the company. Explain policies on vacation and leave, including sick, military, bereavement, personal, family, medical, and jury duty. List paid holidays. State important numbers (such as group insurance numbers or the company code) and email or phone numbers where employees can speak to a benefits representative.

- **Pension or Profit Sharing Plans** – Discuss when and how employees become eligible, whether an employee contribution is permitted or required, and when employees become vested.

- **Standards of Conduct** – This is an important area where you lay down the foundation for acceptable and unacceptable behavior. Add dress code, timeliness, policies on sexual harassment, racial and sexual discrimination, use of alcohol, drugs and tobacco in the workplace (including pre-employment screening and post-accident testing), and disciplinary procedures.

- **Termination** – Here, you will lay out the just causes for which an employee could be fired. This could include criminal activity, poor performance, dishonesty, security breaches, insubordination, absenteeism, company policy violations, health and safety threats, and dress code infractions. Also add the disclaimer that the handbook is not a contract, policies can be changed at any time, and all employment is "at will." This means that the company's relationship with employees is not a guarantee of employment, and can be terminated at any time with or without cause or notice.

- **Employee Relations Procedure** – Create an outline for handling complaints and other issues. This could include a grievance or wage dispute within a union setting, but it also includes such things as discrimination or harassment claims, or any other employee relations issue.

- **General Information** – This might include area maps, a parking pass, an organizational chart, phone lists, a statement regarding the confidential nature of your business, and policies addressing gifts, use of company cars, traffic tickets, email, Internet use, and personal telephone calls. Make sure each new hire gets a copy of the handbook. Have employees sign a statement that they have received and read and fully understand the content. Make updates to your handbook as needed. Make sure you state that all new inclusions override all previous handbooks.

As you think about the topics above, get detailed to cover all aspects. The employee handbook is not a place for generalities. For example, here are some of the points you should discuss

- **Uniforms**: Discuss the entire uniform (headwear, shirts, pants, footwear, cold weather wear, sunglasses, name tags, belt, etc.) Who will supply each part of the uniform? When should they be worn and when should they not be worn? (i.e. sunglasses are good for safe driving but should not be worn when talking to the customer). Who is responsible for cleaning the uniform or replacing parts that are lost or worn out?
- **Telephone use**: Do you provide a company mobile phone for your team? When should they use it and when shouldn't they use it? (For example, the phone shouldn't be used when talking to the customer). What is appropriate usage for personal calls? What is the procedure if the phone is lost or stolen?
- **Vehicle use**: Do you provide a company vehicle? If so, when are they allowed to drive it? Who is responsible for refueling it and how will the fuel be paid and the payment tracked? Who is responsible for maintaining the vehicle? Who is responsible for speeding tickets or parking tickets? How is the vehicle to be kept clean, inside and out?
- **Behavior**: What are the expectations of your employees' behavior? How should an employee communicate (i.e. what kind of language, jokes, or conversation topics are off limits)? What should an employee do if they feel someone else is acting inappropriately?

Employee handbooks can be a daunting project. There are companies that specialize in helping get these done easily for you. You will still need to know what you want to include in the handbook and how you want employees to work in your business, then the handbook company can help move the pieces forward to get the project done. Then, once the heavy lifting is done, you've got your employee handbook (and you can make occasional changes as necessary).

Take Action!

___ Stop doing actions (Actions you currently do now but should stop doing)

_____

_____

___ Keep doing actions (Actions you currently do now and should keep doing)

_____

_____

___ Start doing actions (Actions you don't do now but should start doing)

_____

_____

___ Who will do new actions? (Assign the action to yourself or someone else)

_____

_____

___ By when? (When will these actions be complete?)

_____

_____

POWER KEY #5: HOW TO BECOME A SUPERSTAR MAGNET

Your business grows when you have a team of people that you lead. Unfortunately, many business owners make the mistake of hiring any warm body to do the work. Instead of hiring just anyone, you should commit to hiring only the best and brightest superstars who will help you grow your business.

How do you hire the right people for your team? First, keep in mind that a person's capabilities should always outweigh their actual technical skills. Specific technical skills can be learned and are a fairly common commodity, but a person that actually likes to and wants to learn new things is a rare find.

Look for people who are highly motivated. That doesn't mean they've necessarily achieved a lot in the position they're currently in – sometimes there are other factors that keep someone from ascending in another organization and that's why they want to make a move to your company.

Look for people who work well with others. This new employee should be someone that you feel will fit in well with the team and everyone can work with on a day-to-day basis.

Look for diversity. Don't try to hire people who think just like you do. New ideas will be hard to come by if you surround yourself with drones. Always look for someone who knows more than you do about the specific area for which you are hiring.

Look for employees who are already aligned to your core values and existing company culture (or the one you want to create). Values are also paramount. Make sure that this is a person who will represent you and your organization well. Make sure that this is a person who will do the right thing for your company, the team, and your customers.

Although teamwork is important, make sure the candidate has actually done and is capable of doing work on his own. Ask former coworkers and friends of the candidate what he is like as a worker. Sometimes you are looking for a diamond in the rough – a superstar that just needs a little different training.

Now that you know the qualities of the people you're looking for, let's talk about how to find them.

First, adopt an "always hiring" mentality so that you're not just trying to fill a gap in your team but you're always watching for great people who you can bring on board. Tell people you're always hiring and accepting resumes. I call this "Vending Machine Hiring" because it works just like a vending machine: whenever you need a new employee, you go to your file of resumes and find the best one for the role you're trying to fill. And if you don't have a role to fill right now, that's okay. Accept resumes anyway. That way, if a new position opens up or if you have an employee leave and there's a vacancy, you have a selection of the best candidates to choose from without having to quickly react by advertising for the opening.

Second, be willing to hire for slightly more employees than you actually need. This way of thinking surprises (and perhaps even worries!) most service business owners because they don't want their employees sitting around doing nothing and they don't want to pay for more employees than they need. But if you have slightly more employees than you think you need, you now have a few extra staff hours to help improve your business: you can spend slightly longer serving customers without feeling rushed; you can allow your team to put a little more time to keeping their trucks and your office clean and organized so you position your brand more effectively, you'll be able to put your team to work doing additional marketing for you, and you now have the capacity to take on even more work. (As an added bonus, you'll feel even more motivated to find more work for your team because of the added employee commitments you've made). Hiring slightly more employees than you think you need is a way to help you grow your business… and be ready when your business does grow.

Strategies To Find Great People

The most effective strategy to find great people is to be the company that people want to work at. If you have a negative culture or even if you're just like every other company out here, you won't attract the best employees. So you need to make a cultural shift in your company to create one that prospective employees want to work at. In doing so, you'll completely change the game in how your hiring processes work – people will come out of the woodwork because they want to work for you, and you'll have a wider field of great candidates to choose from. I'll cover more about this in an upcoming chapter.

Another strategy to find great people is to stop relying solely on the standard Help Wanted ad in your local newspaper. Go wider: advertise on job posting sites on the Internet, and access resume databases.

And, encourage current employees to mention openings to their friends and peers. Existing employees will find the best employees sometimes. Offer incentives to your team can give them extra motivation to recommend someone they know.

I use a very powerful, very attractive hiring method in my business: we have "hiring nights" where we invite dozens of prospective candidates into a large room and we share about the company and we watch how people act and react in a large crowd. You can read more about this in my book *The Secrets Of Business Mastery*.

Recruiting is an ongoing task that never ends. You should always be building a future hot list so treat recruiting with its own plan and own hiring budget.

Take Action!

__ Stop doing actions (Actions you currently do now but should stop doing)

_____

_____

__ Keep doing actions (Actions you currently do now and should keep doing)

_____

_____

__ Start doing actions (Actions you don't do now but should start doing)

_____

_____

__ Who will do new actions? (Assign the action to yourself or someone else)

_____

_____

__ By when? (When will these actions be complete?)

_____

_____

POWER KEY #6: THE SURPRISING REASONS WHY PEOPLE WORK FOR YOU

Business owners often see hiring as a type of selling: The potential employee is selling you on why they should work for you and you are selling them on why they should work for you. Both you and the employee need to bring your very best to the forefront to show the other person why you're a good fit for each other. And while that might be technically true, I tend to avoid the words "sales" and "selling" because of the transactional nature of those words and I prefer to talk about serving.

Hiring is a type of serving: The potential employee is thinking about how they can serve you, and you need to think about how you can serve your employees. For example, if a new employee wants to put their kids through college, you can show them how a job at your company can help them do that. When you serve, the selling stops and the mutually beneficial relationship of service begins!

So how do you attract the very best team that you can afford? You do it by identifying all the advantages and benefits that they will gain by working for you.

Note: Although pay is important to most people, don't make the mistake of thinking that you can't afford the very best team and therefore you'll lose them to bigger, higher-paying companies. Pay *is* important but it's only one of several reasons that people work for a company. (For example: An employee who desires rapid advancement to a management level would be able to achieve that faster at a smaller company where their talents and contribution will be noticed more clearly).

Consider some of the following things you might be able to offer prospective employees.

- **Money**: This is often thought to be the first and most important point for any potential employee. Although it's important, it's not always the most important consideration. If you're a smaller company and can't afford to match or beat the offers of larger corporations, that's okay. Make sure you know what you can afford and are willing to pay for the best candidate before you find one. If you are vague about what you can pay going into a negotiation, you're already at a disadvantage and will probably pay too much.

- **Benefits**: Whatever other benefits you provide – such as health insurance, savings plans, etc. – make sure candidates are aware of them and understand how they work.

- **Incentive Programs**: These are ways for your employees to make more money (or earn some other kind of special prize). For example, a commission is a great way for you to provide more money to employees while tying it to the income that is being generated for your company – the more your company makes, the more your employee makes. But it's not just about the money: You might offer gifts, time off, vacations, or other incentives that can be earned through specific actions and achievements.

- **Passion and Philosophy**: Don't underestimate the fact that you are a small business, or feel you need to make an excuse for it. Small size can actually work to your advantage: the excitement and enthusiasm in a small business is usually higher because you are in direct contact with the people who have brought their passion to the table, the owners. Make sure candidates see how passionate you are about your business.

- **Geography**: Geography is another great reason why some people pass up opportunities from higher-paying, larger companies and work for smaller companies; because they can be near family or a school that their kids enjoy. If you are recruiting nationally or internationally and expecting someone to relocate to your area, prepare an extensive list of local benefits and information: housing, schools, shopping, restaurants, attractions, demographics, sports teams, parks, daycares, and community programs will all be important to candidates.

- **Premises**: What type of office will your employee be working from? Make sure you are providing an appealing work environment.

- **Schedule**: Are you offering flexible hours? If you are able to accommodate flexible work schedules for some employees, this can be a great attribute. Offering flexible hours to mothers who have children in school may bring you qualified applicants who might not otherwise apply. Moms will appreciate the opportunity to be at home in the mornings to see the children off to school, and to be there when they arrive home. By advertising these kinds of hours, you might attract highly qualified employees who were not considering going back to work. You will have little or no competition for these candidates. Students often make good employees. Offering flexible schedules and advertising at the local college could bring you a pool of talent from which to choose.

- **Education**: Offering to pay for continuing education is a great way to attract people. Make sure the subjects or courses are related to your business and establish an employment period before you start paying for schooling.
- **Opportunity for future advancement**: In small businesses, growth is usually much faster and advancement opportunity is greater. If this is a possible option in your business, make that known to applicants. With the right future advancement opportunities in place, you will attract highly motivated employees who want to do well and who want their work to be noticed so they can advance quickly. (If this is the kind of approach you want to take in your business, be sure to avoid advancing people based on how long they've been with the company and instead advance people based on measurable performance).
- **Culture**: Culture can be an attractive quality to employees, especially a positive culture of teamwork where everyone's contribution is appreciated.
- **Mission**: Even the mission of the company can attract people. Google's motto "don't be evil" was a humorous and surprising motto about how it would fulfill its mission of organizing the world's information. That mission alone likely attracted many of its employees who wanted a company that thought differently about how to run a business.

It doesn't matter how big your company is. You can attract superstars with the right mix of motivating incentives that serve them.

Take Action!

___ Stop doing actions (Actions you currently do now but should stop doing)

_____

_____

___ Keep doing actions (Actions you currently do now and should keep doing)

_____

_____

__ Start doing actions (Actions you don't do now but should start doing)

_____

_____

__ Who will do new actions? (Assign the action to yourself or someone else)

_____

_____

__ By when? (When will these actions be complete?)

_____

_____

POWER KEY #7: KEEPING SCORE

When you add employees to your team, you expect them to show up on time each day and do their job.

But what is their job and how do you communicate that to them? You might hire a plumber and assume they are qualified to do the work of a plumber but there are still many other aspects of the job that they need to know from you – such as you expect them to act and what you expect them to say when they're talking to customers. The actual trade work might be the same from one company to another but the marketing, serving, and interaction will be different for your company than they are for any others.

As a leader, you need to clearly spell out exactly what your employees should do. Some of this will be done through your employee handbook, discussed earlier. And, most companies create a job description and expect their staff to work within the scope of that description. But this is not a perfect solution.

The problem is, job descriptions are written very generally and are often only referred to during the hiring and onboarding process and then never again afterward. Employees don't really go home at night and re-read their job description to ensure that they are doing the work expected of them.

This creates a challenge: Your employee's definition of the work required of them is unmeasurable and open to interpretation. And worse: their understanding of what is important for them to do on a daily basis comes from what they may (or may not) have initially read when they were first hired, and even more-so from what they see other people doing day-to-day.

Their job description might explain that they need to provide good service to your customers but it probably doesn't go into exact, scripted detail. Who fills in that knowledge gap? Probably the employees they shadow at the very beginning of their employment with your company. Even if they shadow great employees, they'll still only get that employee's interpretation of what is expected of them.

But probably most alarming is: what happens if they act in an undesirable way? They may be able to fall back on the excuse that they weren't told whether or not they could take that undesirable action.

Simply put, you need to clearly spell out exactly what you want them to do. And even more than that, you need to measure their performance regularly so that both you and they can assess how they are doing.

You can do this by creating scorecards for every role in your organization.

A scorecard is a list of specific, measurable tasks and Key Performance Indicators (KPIs) that are tied to the work each employee does, and to your company's core values.

The scorecard should also be color-coded – green when scores are above average, yellow when scores are average, red when scores are below average.

Every week, the employee will get their scorecard with updated numbers that explain how they're doing.

Imagine the difference that this create in your company! Instead of a job description that is open to interpretation, and is really only referred to during the hiring and onboarding process, your employees receive a clear, measurable list of the exact tasks that they are measured on, and they receive this each and every week.

Scorecards reinforce your expectations of the work required, and gauge your employees on how they're doing. It's a measurable way to assess your team. Scorecards are the DNA of your team: It's the "code that embeds a good work ethic into your team and creates a life force that propels your team toward success. It eliminates the guesswork that you have about what they're actually doing while on customer calls, and it eliminates the guesswork that each employee has about what they're doing.

When things are going well, scorecards give you a measurable way to assess who the top performers are (without showing favoritism by ranking based on unclear measurements). With scorecards you can more effectively celebrate your employees' wins.

If your team is struggling and making mistakes and not living up to what you want them to do, it's much harder to start a conversation when you have to say, "remember that job description you read when you started a couple of years ago?" With a scorecard, the conversation is so much easier and straightforward: "Your KPIs were green across the board for a while and suddenly they've gone yellow and now they're red. What's going on and how can we find a solution?"

Scorecards are also very powerful because they help to align the employee with their own job targets as well as the targets of the company. It reveals to them (without any room for excuse or interpretation) where their strong and weak points are, and you'll quickly spot the top performers because they'll want to see their scorecards and they'll work hard to strengthen all areas where they are scored.

Don't make the mistake of looking at scorecards as just another piece of administration that you have to do. They are actually a very powerful tool that helps you lead your team more effectively. In fact, you'll spend less time managing your team and more time leading with scorecards.

Take Action!

__ Stop doing actions (Actions you currently do now but should stop doing)

_____

_____

__ Keep doing actions (Actions you currently do now and should keep doing)

_____

_____

__ Start doing actions (Actions you don't do now but should start doing)

_____

_____

__ Who will do new actions? (Assign the action to yourself or someone else)

_____

_____

__ By when? (When will these actions be complete?)

_____

_____

POWER KEY #8: HOW <u>NOT</u> TO BE LIKE A BOSS

The word "boss" has a bad reputation. Although you are technically the boss, it's not something you want to flaunt. The concept of "boss" has all kinds of negative connotations associated with it. Rather than thinking of yourself as a boss or trying to be like one, be a leader. Don't boss your team; lead them.

So what does it mean to lead? Leadership is not just not just about telling your people what to do. Leadership is really about identifying what your business promises to your customers and then equipping your team to hit that target. And, leadership is about seeing how your business can grow and helping you work in a way that moves the business in that direction of growth.

Leaders lead. They also make it very easy to follow by paving the direction to the target. They also facilitate an environment that lets people on the team grow. A leader doesn't need to drag their team toward success; rather, they point the way and inspire the team to run toward success.

Remember the example I gave earlier in this book about the boat propelled by rowers? Your team is like the rowers in a boat. They cannot see where they are going; they are only focused on their oar. But you, as the leader, are looking forward and helping your team work together to move the boat in the right direction.

There are four basic situations in the workplace where you will have to interact with your employees.

- If the employees under your leadership are not willing or able to do the job at hand, you must tell them what to do and how to do it.
- When employees are willing and know how to complete a task, you can respond by delegating the appropriate tasks to the appropriate people.
- Employees who have the ability to do a job but need a little guidance as to how to go about it may respond well to a participatory setting in which their input is considered in the decision making process.
- Finally, if the employees under your leadership are willing to undertake a project but have no idea how to go about it, you will then have to demonstrate the skills necessary for the task at hand and elicit volunteers to accomplish each assignment.

What overall method do you use to lead your employees? None of us are born with a particular style of leading others, and we can develop one that works best for us and for those around us. Different occasions will demand different styles of leadership, and the flexibility to change from one style to another can be very important.

Finding the right style that works for you and for your team is important. Remember: employees rarely quit companies; they always quit managers first.

You'll also find that your leadership style must grow as your company grows. At first, you might lead one or two employees. Then one or two teams of employees. Then leaders of teams. As you change who you are leading, your leadership style will need to evolve as well. Fortunately, you don't have to use the "trial and error" method to evolve your leadership style: work with a mentor or coach to help you develop your leadership skills and styles.

Here are the components that make up your leadership style:

Hands-on versus hands-off: Some leaders are hands-on, showing their team how to do something and then working alongside them as they do it. This approach is useful in the very beginning, while getting new employees up-to-speed with what is expected of them to complete the task in the way they need it completed. Later, though, as they gain experience, you should step back and allow them to do the job themselves. But you will continue to lead. Avoid the temptation to micromanage work that your employees do. (Instead, use the scorecards discussed in a previous chapter to monitor their work). Transitioning from hands-on to hands-off leadership requires that you have thoroughly trained your team and that you trust them.

Communication: Leaders tell their team what is expected and give them the instruction and encouragement required to complete the job. Work at communicating clearly so your employees know exactly what is expected. Instructions should be detailed.

Your own personality will come out in your communication (sometimes that's a good thing and sometimes it's not!) If you are naturally a quiet person, you'll need to open up a bit to become a more vocal communicator. If you are naturally an outgoing person, you'll need to monitor your communication to ensure that you are keeping your communication on-track.

Reporting requirements: Another component of your leadership style is your requirement for reporting. Who reports on the progress of a project, task, or activity? How often? What information do they need to provide? You'll want enough reports to know what's going on (so you don't get any surprises) but not so many that you are micromanaging.

Take Action!

__ Stop doing actions (Actions you currently do now but should stop doing)

_____

_____

__ Keep doing actions (Actions you currently do now and should keep doing)

_____

_____

__ Start doing actions (Actions you don't do now but should start doing)

_____

_____

__ Who will do new actions? (Assign the action to yourself or someone else)

_____

_____

__ By when? (When will these actions be complete?)

_____

_____

POWER KEY #9: BATTLE OF THE CHROMOSOME: GENDER AND LEADERSHIP

A lot is written about the differences between men and women. Unfortunately, too much time is spent on exploring which of the differences are superior. I am not interested in identifying which type of leadership is better because I've found that although men and women think and act differently, they each bring something valuable to the leader's role.

There are considerable differences between men and women in leadership. Whether these differences are the result of nature (how we're born) or nurture (how we're raised) is up for debate. I think it's a mix of those two.

I've seen great male leaders and great female leaders and I think both men and women can learn something from great male and female leaders.

Understanding and effectively navigating these differences is what I want to focus on for this chapter. The service industry is largely dominated by men so understanding how men and women lead differently will help you to work well with anyone, regardless of their gender.

Male leaders tend to use a more directive leadership style that is focused on the goals (sometimes will less regard for the people who will working toward the goal). On the other hand, female leaders involve a more participative leadership style and generally have more empathy and sympathy for others. Women tend to lead with a democratic style, whereas men lead using an autocratic, directive style.

The interactive leadership style common among women encourages participation and the sharing of power and information. For men, there is participation but it's not necessarily actively sought out.

There are plenty of other differences between the typical leadership style of each gender, including:

- Women seem to nurture and promote the development of subordinates.
- Men lead from a viewpoint of competition, confrontation and conflict.
- Women seek harmony while men seek control.
- Men view power as dominance over others.

- Women usually see power as increased responsibility and use their power in a win-win manner to help others.
- Men see conflict as part of leadership and are openly competitive.
- Women see conflict as personal and in a negative and disruptive light.
- Women often use a transformational leadership style in the interest of pursuing a common target.
- Men often demonstrate a transactional leadership style using structural power to reward and punish.

I should also note here that we are talking about generalities: Even within male leadership or female leadership there will still be a spectrum. Some male leaders are more nurturing than other male leaders; some female leaders are more competitive than other female leaders. My focus in this chapter is not so much to identify all the exact differences that exist between men and women but rather to show that there are general patterns to leadership styles and those patterns are often (although not always) associated with gender.

Again, I'm not suggesting that one way is better. There are good qualities to learn from both. More importantly, understanding that there is a difference in the way we communicate with everyone is very important.

Complications arise when we're used to one type of leader and we are being led by a different type. Here's an example that you should be aware of because it may happen in your business: if one of your teams always worked for a male manager and then that manager moved out the position and was replaced by a female manager, the dynamic of the team would change because the leadership style was dramatically different. As the company leader, you should be aware of that before the change is completed and work to address it – not by asking the new team member to change their leadership style but by working with the team to show them that the new leader's style is different but just as important to follow.

Whether leading a team or communicating among your peers, all communication should be aligned and agreed upon in the beginning with the awareness that there are different styles, and each style has value to add. It's also essential to make sure that the leader fits both the existing culture and the culture you desire to have.

The simplest way to navigate the complexities of leadership and gender in your workplace is this: understand that there is a difference between how men and women lead (and even differences within the leadership style of each gender) and yet we always expect that employees respect every leader.

Take Action!

__ Stop doing actions (Actions you currently do now but should stop doing)

_____

_____

__ Keep doing actions (Actions you currently do now and should keep doing)

_____

_____

__ Start doing actions (Actions you don't do now but should start doing)

_____

_____

__ Who will do new actions? (Assign the action to yourself or someone else)

_____

_____

__ By when? (When will these actions be complete?)

_____

_____

POWER KEY #10: PERFORMANCE-ENHANCING COMMUNICATION!

Do you ever feel that nobody gets it? Do you get tired of always trying to clarify the meaning of what you said, or apologizing for not saying what you meant? If this keeps happening, perhaps it's worth looking at the way you are delivering your message.

Communication would be simple if we could get exactly our idea across to the person we're communicating with, without any breakdown in meaning. But that's not how it works.

You may have an idea in your mind of something you want to say but that idea is limited by the words you use. And the person who hears those words then needs to interpret the words into the idea in their own minds. So there are several points in the process when your idea can potentially become very different than the idea that is understood by the hearer.

And to add to that complexity, communication is only partly what we say; it's also how we say it. Slight inflections in your voice can make the same sentence sound like a command, a suggestion, or a question – and each of those will get very different results.

If communication isn't complex enough already, research shows that people retain only 10 percent of what they hear 72 hours after hearing it.

How do you ensure that you effectively communicate your ideas, ensure that your team understands those ideas, and ensure that they follow through correctly?

Here are some strategies to be a better communicator:

- Eliminate distractions. Turn off cell phones in a meeting. Focus just on the people you are communicating with. When possible, meet in a quiet place.

- Spend a few moments preparing what you need to say before you say it. If necessary, practice or even get someone to listen and give you feedback. The more important your communication will be, and the bigger the group you'll be communicating to, the more you should prepare.

- Remember that communication is a two-way street: You are speaking and you should also listen.

- Be an empathic listener. Put yourself in each person's shoes.

Remember the analogy of a ship captain relying on his oarsmen to keep the boat moving while he navigated? All of your planning will be a waste of time if your oarsmen, or employees, do not know which way they should be rowing, are not motivated to row, or stop rowing. Effective communication is the key to relaying direction.

Besides communication with your employees, though, there is another type of communication happening that can reduce or even halt productivity. This is the communication among your employees. One estimate is that over 16 hours of a week per employee is lost in the average company due to lack of employee communication and the subsequent fallout. That is equal to almost half of an average workweek! Poor communication may include misunderstandings, inappropriate chatter, manipulation, personal correspondence through chatrooms and email, social gathering plans for outside work, gossip, and news and events and other non-work-related talk.

You cannot control everything other people are talking about, but you can instill a professional work attitude, plan and delegate enough work to keep employees busy, and monitor as much as possible. Consider whom you will be communicating with. What do you know about your employees? For instance:

- **Educational Background** - What is the person's level and type of education? Are you choosing vocabulary he understands? Are you talking beneath him?
- **Lifestyle** – Do you know the person's lifestyle? Avoid making any assumptions about people that could lead to offensive comments.
- **Life Experience** – Communicating with a 21-year-old person can be very different than talking with a 55-year-old. With experience should come patience, comprehension, and hopefully some wisdom. People relate new ideas and information to past experiences.
- **Ethnicity** – We all work with people from various cultures and backgrounds. There may be specific terms or cultural vernacular the person does not understand, or certain things he says that you do not understand.
- **Geography** – Where is the person from or where has he grown up?
- **Gender** – Men and women relate to others in different ways. Our society has accepted certain expectations of gender roles and behaviors that are interweaved into communication. The identities formed for gender dictate how we communicate with each other.

Gender is an important consideration for communication because each sex views each other in dissimilar ways. Men and women behave and interpret situations differently.

- **Relationship** – The relationship you have with a person is critical to conversation. How does this person see you?

- **Personality** – Factor in the personality of an employee when you meet with him. Do what you can to get to know each person better so you can communicate better.

- **Past Behavior** – If you know how someone has reacted to situations in the past, this is a good indicator of how he will react in the future.

After you have assessed the person you will be communicating with, consider how to put your message in his terms. Contemplate his vocabulary, listening ability, and pattern of thinking. Some people cannot handle more than a few simple instructions at once.

These hold true for you, as well: these factors will determine what you say and how you say, and how you understand what other people are saying. The better you understand yourself, the better you'll appreciate that others are not like you.

Now consider your method of communication. Some people respond better to verbal instructions, others a written message, while still other people need both. Ask people to repeat your instructions or communication back to you. You can do this without sounding condescending by saying something like this: "I'm not sure if I really communicated that well, could you tell me what I just said?" You might get some surprising responses, but this exercise gives you the opportunity to head off misunderstandings before they become counterproductive.

Everyone has filters through which they hear and interpret information. These filters include their level of vocabulary and language, their personal self-image, past experiences, their perception of you, and expectations. Don't assume anything when communicating with others. Remember to listen well. Most miscommunication can be attributed to poor listening.

If you're still having trouble communicating with employees, try a few of the following ideas:

- **Battling Opposition** – When met with opposition to your ideas try using creative vocabulary to better explain them.

- **Disarm People** – How can you make people more receptive to your message? Whenever possible, set the mood, or control the environment where you communicate. People in a relaxed state of mind are more receptive to listening. Start conversations in a relaxed or neutralizing manner. While many managers and business owners feel chitchat is a waste of time, this can disarm people and put them in a receptive state. In addition, you will often get more and useful information from people when chatting. A defensive person usually has reduced listening ability. They will not hear most of what you say. A person on the defensive will stop at the words they find offensive. You will waste an incredible amount of time breaking down someone in this state.

- **Allow Time for Questions** – In addition to having people repeat your instructions or statements, ask them if they have questions. If you're in a group setting, also allow private time for one-on-one questions from individuals involved in the group. You could also let them ask questions via email. People will often be willing to discuss things privately that they would not ask in a group setting because they do not want to appear less intelligent in front of their peers. Follow up with people and ask if they need assistance or have questions about a project or task.

- **Make it easy to find information and to review** – Record your communication with video – it's an easy way to preserve what you have to say so people can go back and review later.

- **Share these strategies with your team**. Don't keep these strategies secret from the rest of your team; share them so that everyone is on board. By teaching everyone on your team these strategies, they will then understand what you are doing and be aligned with what is expected at your company.

Take Action!

___ Stop doing actions (Actions you currently do now but should stop doing)

_____

_____

__ Keep doing actions (Actions you currently do now and should keep doing)

_____

_____

__ Start doing actions (Actions you don't do now but should start doing)

_____

_____

__ Who will do new actions? (Assign the action to yourself or someone else)

_____

_____

__ By when? (When will these actions be complete?)

_____

_____

POWER KEY #11: PROJECT-SPECIFIC COMMUNICATION STRATEGIES

The projects you and your team work on – whether they are a small project for a customer or a large one, or any other task you might ask your team to perform on the job – these projects don't always go as planned.

One of the most frustrating aspects of projects is the difference between expectations and results. You ask for, and expect, one outcome but your team delivers something else. Perhaps they don't deliver it to your standards or in the timeframe you asked for or the outcome is completely different altogether.

Most often, this is due to a lack of communication or to misunderstood or poor communication. It's easy to lay the blame of the inadequate result upon those who did the work but the truth is: the leader must accept most of the blame for not properly explaining exactly what needed to be done.

How do you effectively communicate to your team so they complete a project within your requirements and expectations? In a previous chapter I laid out the groundwork for good communication. In this chapter I want to help you apply it to specific projects (or even simple tasks) that you ask your team to do. Think of this chapter as the practical application of the communication principles I've been discussing so far, applied to many of the day-to-day activities you ask your team to do.

Here's how to get your team completing projects and tasks to your expectations:

First, projects need to be clearly defined. Projects fall into three categories, which I define like as boulders, rocks, and stones:

- **Boulders** are big-ass projects that will make huge changes and impacts and may take six months or less.
- **Rocks** are middle-sized projects that will be complete in three months or less.
- **Stones** are smaller projects that will be complete in 30 days or less.
- Anything less than 30 days is just a **task** to get done.

Defining what kind of project you're looking at achieving will help you with the next steps…

Second, projects need to be clearly articulated to your team.
Projects need to be clearly articulated to your team before they start. If I
need to purchase some equipment for the office and I ask a team member
to go to the store to purchase it, the project might seem clear enough but I
haven't asked the team member to return right to the office and set it up for
me. The employee has technically completed the task if they go to the store,
buy the item, and then take off for the rest of the day to watch TV in their
living room. Was the project successful in my eyes? No. Was the project
successful in the employee's eyes? Technically yes because they did exactly
what I asked.

This example would, of course, be grounds for a very serious discussion
with the employee but I put it here to illustrate in a humorous way the
difference between expectations and outcomes as a result of
communication.

Describe what you desire as the outcome of the project as clearly as
possible. If the project requires a process then you may need to describe the
steps and any other parameters first. In the example above, a better
description would have included the employee returning to the office and
setting up the equipment. And I might also need to give the specific
parameters of the price I want paid for the purchase or the brand I want or
the store to purchase from, since the employee might simply go to the
nearest store because it's convenient or the farthest store because they want
to take a leisurely drive. So clear definitions are required up-front on any
aspect of the project that might be open to interpretation.

Along with going through the specific project with the team, another
strategy is to work with the person leading the project and review any
decision-making criteria with them. For example, if the project requires a
number of decisions, help them understand which decisions can be decided
by them and which ones need to be decided by someone else, and when
they're in charge of a decision, help them to know how to make the right
decisions that will align with the company's core values and purpose, and
with the targets of the project.

Third, projects need to be agreed upon before any work is done.
You and your team need to agree that this project is the right thing to do,
and you need to agree on who will manage the individual pieces that make
up the project. This is also a great opportunity for your employees to make
recommendations or alert you to any challenges they might have in
completing the task. Seeking agreement with your team about the deadlines
and who is in charge gets the whole team aligned (and it's a very different
approach than how many companies do the work – with one person
barking orders and everyone else scurrying to complete those orders).

Seeking agreement does not mean that you are running a democracy where everyone gets to vote on whether the project needs to be done. Rather, the agreement is more like alignment and a checkpoint to ensure that everyone understands and agrees that the project and its requirements can be completed as directed.

Fourth, projects should have a platform where status updates can be posted so everyone is aligned on progress. This platform might be a meeting at the very beginning or end of the day where people connect briefly to give status reports; it might be a 5-minute conference call where people dial in remotely from wherever they are; it might be a software tool where participants check-in and report on their progress (it doesn't have to be a complex project management software – even a tool like Google Docs or shared access to a spreadsheet on Dropbox can work). Use any combination of the platforms that make the most sense for you. Avoid using email as a project management tool because it doesn't provide clear enough visibility to enable true leadership of a project.

Fifth, projects need to have different levels of leadership, depending on the size of the project. A smaller project might be handed off to a leader at a lower level while a major project that impacts all levels of the organization should receive leadership from the executive team. Select the appropriate level of leadership for the project based on the scope of change that the project will create. Even in a small company it's important that you empower the leaders under you to handle the projects that are appropriate for their level. Avoid the temptation to lead those projects too. You may show up at the very beginning to help communicate the project's importance, and of course you'll get regular updates from the project leader, but otherwise you should be hands off.

Sixth, you need to trust your team. Projects are best completed if you trust the people you have tasked with the work. Micromanaging will not get the task done faster. Micromanagement happens when a leader doesn't describe a project's outcome effectively or doesn't trust the team to complete the work. You will instantly get more time in your day if you take the time up-front to build a team that is qualified, trained, and who you trust, and if you explain the requirements of each project effectively.

(Note: micromanaging is the first sign of weak leadership. True leaders should be concerned with how to lead and communicate effectively.)

Seventh, evaluate the project at the end. When the project draws to a close, make sure you collect lessons learned so that you understand what went well on the project and what could have been improved. Use those lessons to improve future projects.

Take Action!

__ Stop doing actions (Actions you currently do now but should stop doing)

_____

_____

__ Keep doing actions (Actions you currently do now and should keep doing)

_____

_____

__ Start doing actions (Actions you don't do now but should start doing)

_____

_____

__ Who will do new actions? (Assign the action to yourself or someone else)

_____

_____

__ By when? (When will these actions be complete?)

_____

_____

POWER KEY #12: HOW TO GIVE DIRECTION AND GUIDANCE

In an earlier chapter I explained why it's important to give a clear explanation of a project's outcome. It's one of the first steps to ensure that any project – small or large – is done to your satisfaction and most business and leadership failure happens when this isn't done properly.

Now I want to explore that concept just a little further to help you give clear directions. No matter what the project, task, or job is, giving directions effectively will help the project be completed the way it should.

Unfortunately, many service business owners fall into one of two camps when it comes to giving directions:

- Some leaders give orders rather than direction. They tell their employees what they want them to do, verbally walking the employee step-by-step through the process. "Go here, then do this, then do this, this do this."

- Some leaders don't give enough direction. They give a vague description of what they want done and then they let the employee figure it out.

Both of these methods have drawbacks: giving orders to your employees requires them to respond in the prescribed manner and gives no room for them to figure out what they think is the best way to handle the task. You, as a leader, are not letting your employees learn. You are limiting them to your level of expertise. You are setting the bar too low for what you expect of your employees by making it seem that as long as they follow the steps at the bare minimum, they will keep their job.

And on the other hand, giving too little direction creates just as many problems: it leaves too much room for doubt and error. You are not letting your employees learn because they're faced with a mountain of decisions they need to make and not enough guidance to know how to make those decisions. You are setting the bar too high for what you expect of your employees.

A more effective way to complete a project is to give direction. Give instructions or guidelines, clearly explain the desired outcome, and allow your team to complete the work.

Giving direction means:

- Describing the ideal outcome of the work you want done and explaining what a successful completion looks like.
- Outlining any mission-critical steps that should be followed.
- Anticipating problems and questions and roadblocks your team might experience and addressing those.

I mentioned earlier that giving *orders* was giving all the steps that they will face. Giving *directions* leaves some room for the employee to complete some steps themselves. However, there will be times when you have to give certain specific steps – perhaps for safety or because that's the way you want all your staff to complete a particular project. (For example, in my company, we have a Framework for Service which is a sequence that our team follows when serving customers, and the team is given these steps and required to follow them in sequence). However, only the most mission-critical steps should be given.

There are definite benefits to not telling an employee exactly how to complete every step of a project. When an employee is given direction instead of orders, he must invest a little bit of himself in finding a solution to the problem. There is always a chance that he will come up with a better solution than the one you had in mind. Also, if the employee has come up with the method of accomplishing the task, he will believe that the solution is a good one and will defend it to others. The more self-ownership you can allow your team to take on, the better all projects get done.

Although it might be tempting for you to fall into the habit of giving orders or not giving enough direction at all, this method of giving quality directions will help you: you will end up with happier employees who do great work (which reduces employee turnover and also leads to happier customers), and, you won't have to go back and "fix" projects that were not adequately completed the first time. Simply put: giving good directions up-front may require slightly more time up-front but ultimately creates better results and gives you more time to work on your business.

You should be aware that this kind of direction takes practice. It will not happen overnight. Practice giving good directions, and perhaps even find someone to work with you to listen as you give directions and then to give you feedback on the effectiveness of those directions. The skill of giving good directions will directly result in more time for you to focus on your business.

This is not a control issue! Many owners believe they will grow their business when they maintain tight control, and by giving directions instead of orders they are giving up control. But in reality those businesses never grow – they stagnate because the owner is so busy giving orders and then correcting the team.

The last piece of the puzzle in this Power Key is the methodology you use to give direction and guidance. Fortunately, there are many technologies available for you to use to give direction and guidance effectively. Some of the ways I use include:

- Face-to-face meetings – whether larger organizational meetings or quick stand-up "touchpoint" meetings at the beginning or end of the day.
- Teleseminars – where people dial in (which works well if you need to align and communicate with a remote team.
- Webinars – this is good if you have a remote team, if you plan to have some discussion, and if you have visuals you'd like to share.
- Videos – these are powerful and very fast to produce and they're a great way to communicate something out to your team.
- Leadership emails – use these when you have something important to communicate and want to direct the team. Be careful how you manage replies because you don't want to have project discussions on email. Use these more for directives and instruction, and you may want to use these emails for people to make individual replies, but this is not the tool for discussion.
- Leadership text – use this tool when you have something short to share, such as an encouragement or brief discussion.

All of these tools are great ways to lead efficiently. However, make sure you select the right method for the kind of instruction/discussion/feedback you hope to achieve.

Ending your micromanagement and trusting your team will empower them – that's the kind of team you want. And communicating effectively with your team will get them moving forward in the right way.

And, of course, you'll ultimately change what your daily schedule looks like too – with the right leadership strategies, you'll have more time to work on your business instead of in your business!

Take Action!

__ Stop doing actions (Actions you currently do now but should stop doing)

_____

_____

__ Keep doing actions (Actions you currently do now and should keep doing)

_____

_____

__ Start doing actions (Actions you don't do now but should start doing)

_____

_____

__ Who will do new actions? (Assign the action to yourself or someone else)

_____

_____

__ By when? (When will these actions be complete?)

_____

_____

POWER KEY #13: AVOID THESE CATASTROPHIC LEADERSHIP BLUNDERS

As a leader, you put yourself out there every day, working to inspire and motivate your team and point them toward the vision you have of your successful company.

The work of a leader is hard work, which is why so many business owners default into other forms of management (ignoring, barely giving any direction, or micromanaging). These other default management styles seem easier than leading but they're really not – they ultimately put more work on your shoulders.

Leading is hard work but leading is also the style that will give you more time to grow your business.

As you lead, you'll face a multitude of interactions with your employees, your vendors, your customers, your prospective employees, and others, and every interaction runs the risk that you'll make one or more of these leadership and communication blunders.

Here are some of the most common communication issues you may run into as a leader. I've discussed some of them in this book already, and others are mentioned here as a brief caution against committing them:

- **Giving poor instructions**: As I've explained throughout this book, giving good, clear instructions will help your employees do the right work and it will free up your time to focus on your work.
- **Inability to listen to instructions**: Yes, even leaders get instruction. You might be a manager who works for the owner. Even as an owner you might receive instructions from someone else, such as an accountant or attorney who needs to you to complete a specific action, or from a mentor or consultant who is advising you on a change to make in your business.
- **Causing personal/emotional discord**: Leaders rarely intentionally do this but it does happen and it can tear apart a business very quickly. You can avoid it by getting to know your employees, understanding their motivations, and learning about their personality styles.
- **Inciting anger**: Surprisingly (and disappointingly) this happens from managers (I don't want to use the term "leaders" here) who use anger as a source of motivation. It's ineffective at motivating a team… it's far more effective at increasing employee turnover.

- **Miscommunication of ideas**: As I've explained earlier in this book, communicating our ideas clearly will create better work from your team.
- **Revealing proprietary information**: Some aspects of your business need to remain private, even from your employees. Understand what can be shared and how is qualified to know.
- **Irrelevant communication**: Irrelevant communication is unproductive and distracting and keeps your team from performing at their best. (Note: I'm not necessarily talking about friendly conversation, which can be used at appropriate times to build rapport).
- **Counterproductive communication**: Communication that does not build people up or move projects forward is counterproductive. It could be anything from deceiving employees to telling dirty jokes. Only ever communicate in a way that builds people up and moves projects forward.
- **Not sharing the whole agenda**: When you have a meeting, share the whole agenda ahead of time. This helps people understand what the meeting is about, arrive prepared, and know how long the meeting will be. Failing to share the agenda keeps people in the dark and reduces participation.
- **Correcting others**: Your job as a leader includes providing correction, and there is a time and place for it. Avoid correcting your employees publicly in a way that would embarrass them, and be sure to balance your correction with constructive advice and praise.
- **Trying to control others**: You hire employees to work for you; you don't hire clones. Avoid micromanaging and controlling your team. Build a good team, train them well, empower them with the tools and strategies, and then trust them to do a good job.
- **Pushing employees to do more than they are capable of or able to do**: It's okay to sometimes encourage an employee to stretch beyond their comfort zone but this should be done carefully. Asking an employee to do more than they are skilled to do could be dangerous, and asking an employee to do more than they are morally able to do is unethical.
- **Changing direction too fast**: As a leader, you see the big picture so it's easy to change direction quickly. But your team doesn't see the picture at the level you do so they need more time.
- **Being unclear about changes that are happening**: Again, you see the whole picture so you know why changes are taking place.

You need to explain these to your employees to help them understand the reason behind any changes they're seeing.

- **Not helping employees grow**: True leadership is all about helping each member of your team ascend to a higher level. Understand how your team members want to grow and help them get there.

- **Ignoring the needs of the employee and only working on what's good for your business**: Although you should expect your team to show up and work hard for the good of the company, you need to understand that they have their own lives that are influencing their thoughts and decisions. Take the time to understand your employees and serve them, and you'll get better work from them.

These leadership and communication blunders are common and easy to commit. Avoiding them will help you lead your team with excellence and create a high-performing team that accelerates your business to new heights.

Take Action!

___ Stop doing actions (Actions you currently do now but should stop doing)

_____

_____

___ Keep doing actions (Actions you currently do now and should keep doing)

_____

_____

__ Start doing actions (Actions you don't do now but should start doing)

_____

_____

__ Who will do new actions? (Assign the action to yourself or someone else)

_____

_____

__ By when? (When will these actions be complete?)

_____

_____

POWER KEY #14: FEEDBACK AND PERFORMANCE INTERVIEWS

Your employees joined your company because they see you and your business as an opportunity to help them achieve their own personal targets in life. As a business owner and manager, it's your job to help them remain aligned to your business and to show them how they can continually improve – improve how they work for you, which improves how you can reward them and help them achieve those targets.

You can help them improve through performance reviews and ongoing feedback – two essential components of the feedback loop that should be used in every business.

Feedback

Feedback is the assessment you give to an employee about their actions and results on the job. It's typically an informal process that happens when the opportunity arises.

Provide feedback on a daily basis. Don't wait for your employee's scheduled performance interview every 90 days to give them feedback. An employee's assessment of their performance should not be a surprise to them! (If they are surprised by what you say then this should alert you to the fact that you're not giving enough measurable daily feedback).

Most feedback should start in the form of a question. This gives the employee a chance to speak and draw conclusions and will provide you with more information.

Feedback is so important that it should be embedded into your culture. Develop in your business a culture that gives and receives plenty of kind but transparent feedback. If this is embedded right in your culture then you avoid building negative attitudes like regret or resentment.

Remember that not all feedback needs to occur when negative actions should be corrected. Be generous with positive feedback, which reinforces good behavior through approval.

Give feedback immediately. The sooner and more frequently you provide employees with feedback, the sooner and more often you'll have information.

Praise your employees publicly and coach them privately: When an employee has a great success, make sure to provide positive feedback about it in front of others. When an employee has struggled at something, provide feedback (coaching) in private so that the employee isn't embarrassed and can put their focus on what they need to learn.

Performance Interviews

Many business owners struggle just to keep up with all the demands on their time that they face each day. From customer issues to employee issues, it can feel like you're treading water… barely!

Therefore, it comes as no surprise that employee reviews can take a backseat to all of the seemingly more pressing priorities in your day.

But I like to think about these differently – and not even call them "employee reviews" at all. "Employee reviews" is a term that has a lot of negativity attached to it, and employees can feel like they're on the chopping block each time. And for you, it can feel like a chore to write out a review for each employee every 3 or 6 months (or less frequently, as is often the case!), and it feels like a chore to deliver the review.

Here's a better way to think about this process: First, rename them "performance interviews," which immediately breaks from the baggage-laden terminology of "employee reviews" and sets up the opportunity to create positive associations with performance reviews.

Second, stop thinking of it as a chore. As a business owner, your main purpose is to serve your customers with excellence and this is a way you can increase the excellent delivery of service from all your staff.

Third, push beyond the present: Performance interviews are like high level coaching and mentoring. They can include next steps for training and also skills about leading. It is about becoming better, not just an assessment of what the employee is doing right now.

Fourth, use the time to solicit feedback from your team. This isn't an employee review any longer, this is a time for a scheduled one-on-one discussion so that both you and your employee can learn from each other and grow.

Of course this process should include documentation, but it shouldn't just be about checking of a list of boxes that rate an employee's competence in various tasks. Rather, it should be about you helping your team become better, and delivering it in a positive, constructive way. Your team will appreciate it and they'll be more loyal because they'll see that you are helping them grow.

Feedback From Employees To You

There's one more kind of feedback – feedback from the employee to you. Be sure to ask your employees for feedback.

This can be done informally or during performance reviews (as I described above). But one of the best ways to get employee feedback is through company-wide surveys, since employees will more likely open up when their feedback is anonymous.

Always keep the lines of communication open in both directions and you will greatly increase productivity.

Always Get Feedback

Feedback that results in change creates maximum power, so always ask for feedback. I mentioned above that you can ask employees for feedback through performance reviews or through company-wide surveys. But you don't have to wait until a specific time to give a survey. Whenever you have an item you want feedback on, you can do an anonymous survey of your employees (or even your peers) to get their feedback and guidance.

Take Action!

___ Stop doing actions (Actions you currently do now but should stop doing)

_____

_____

___ Keep doing actions (Actions you currently do now and should keep doing)

_____

_____

___ Start doing actions (Actions you don't do now but should start doing)

_____

_____

__ Who will do new actions? (Assign the action to yourself or someone else)

_____

_____

__ By when? (When will these actions be complete?)

_____

_____

POWER KEY #15: CONFLICT RESOLUTION SECRETS

A survey conducted among employers in Britain revealed that dealing with disputes cost the average British employer about 350 days of management and Human Resource time every year! That is a lot of time that could be spent doing so many more productive activities. I imagine that the numbers aren't all the different here in the US.

Conflicts will arise in the workplace – whether they are turf wars or personality conflicts – and must be dealt with. As a leader, your job is to create an environment in which your employees feel comfortable and thus able perform at their best. If you are approachable, they will feel comfortable coming to you before going to Human Resources or upper management. However, if you choose not to intervene in conflicts that arise, you will put the positive atmosphere you have worked so hard to create at risk.

Regardless of the size of your company (whether you run a company with a Human Resource department or one that is too small for its own HR department) you need skills to understand and handle conflict and minimize negative conflict altogether.

Conflict is not necessarily a bad thing. Meaningful conflict can help create a healthy, successful business. This surprises most people but we see it is true everywhere we look: even in nature, broken bones grow back stronger, forest fires help clear out the deadwood to make room for new growth, and only the strong animals that survive conflict survive.

In business, similar benefits apply: disagreements are necessary for problem solving and for strengthening relationships. When people are free to disagree, it is more likely that all options for a project will be discussed and that better decisions will be made.

In fact, effective team building exercises are built to help create conflict so it can be resolved.

Unfortunately, rather than recognizing the value and need for constructive conflict, many business owners do whatever they can to avoid conflict. In building a business that avoids conflict, they aren't really avoiding it but are ignoring that it exists (which creates an environment where conflict can become unhealthy).

It's true that conflict can sometimes feel uncomfortable for many people. However, participating in and managing conflict effectively will have positive ramifications. As a leader, your job is to create a workplace atmosphere in which your employees feel comfortable expressing different viewpoints.

The first step toward this target is to make your expectations clear. Your employees should understand that differences of opinion are okay and that you expect them to voice these opinions. Discussion about issues should be the status quo, not the exception. As long as everybody is working toward a common target, there is always more than one way to get there.

Recognize employees who are willing to go against the flow and voice a differing opinion. Thank them for taking a stand. However, make sure that your employees are able to support their recommendations with facts and figures. Disagreeing just to disagree will get you nowhere and personal attacks are never acceptable.

Hire people you believe will add value to your organization by being willing and able to problem solve and debate issues. Behavioral interview questions can aid you in identifying these candidates. Look for someone who is willing to go against the grain and is not worried about his popularity in the workplace. Provide newer and older employees alike with training in healthy conflict resolution and problem solving.

Make sure there is a conflict manager – someone who helps people get past the more challenging conflict that escalates beyond professional disagreement. In my company, we instituted a "stop word" that was used if conflict was starting to get out of hand. When the word was said, everyone would part until the next meeting. Institute a similar practice in your company.

If you experience little dissension in your workplace, look at your own attitudes and actions. Do you send verbal or nonverbal messages that suggest disagreement will not be tolerated? Do you "grill" employees publicly when they suggest completion of a task via different methods than you had originally proposed? Do you punish employees when a solution they had proposed to a problem fails? Discuss with your employees if and why they are reluctant to voice differing opinions. Rectify any problems, including your own attitudes, which may be standing in the way of healthy, constructive work conflict and debate.

What To Do When Conflict Gets Out Of Hand

There will be times that conflicts get out of hand and as a leader you will be required to step in and provide a resolution to the matter in order to preserve workplace harmony. Signs that a conflict has escalated too far include: employees criticizing other staff members, an increase in the number and severity of negative comments, secret meetings among staff members, and email wars.

When you have identified a situation in which you feel you need to step in, there are three things you must avoid doing in your attempt to mediate the disagreement.

First, do not avoid the conflict and hope it will resolve on its own. Most likely, it will not, and, even if the situation does subside, it will resurface whenever stress increases.

Second, do not meet with the parties involved on an individual basis. If you do this, you place yourself in the position of judge and jury, and the parties feel that they must prove themselves to be right. There will be no willingness to compromise.

Third, do not convince yourself that the only people affected by the disagreement are the participants. Disagreements that become out of hand result in a hostile atmosphere and other employees may end up taking sides.

So what should you do if you have to step into the middle of a disagreement? Make it a point to meet with the individuals involved together. Get total transparency into the situation. I call this: "calling the blue elephant 'blue'."

Allow each party to present his case without interruption by the other party. Ask each employee what he would like to see the other employees do differently. You, as a leader, may need to step in at this point and provide the means or give the permission necessary for the desired changes to take place. All participants should discuss and commit to making these changes. Make sure that you remain neutral during this discussion and make it clear to those involved that you expect them to take proactive steps to resolve the conflict within a specific timeframe. Let them know that it is okay to have disagreements over issues and plans, but that it is not okay to let personality conflicts affect the entire organization. If these personal issues continue to be a problem, disciplinary action or dismissal may be called for.

Take Action!

__ Stop doing actions (Actions you currently do now but should stop doing)

_____

_____

__ Keep doing actions (Actions you currently do now and should keep doing)

_____

_____

__ Start doing actions (Actions you don't do now but should start doing)

_____

_____

__ Who will do new actions? (Assign the action to yourself or someone else)

_____

_____

__ By when? (When will these actions be complete?)

_____

_____

POWER KEY #16: HOW TO GET MORE OUT OF YOUR TEAM

There is a lot of literature out there about motivating people. However, I don't actually believe that you can motivate someone. Motivation is internal; it's individual for each person. People can only motivate themselves. Fortunately, you can facilitate an environment to people motivate themselves.

For example:

- Your core promise will inspire people to work for your company because of what you, as a business, desire to achieve.
- Your culture can be one where everyone sees themselves as part of a team; therefore, people will feel motivated to work so that they help elevate the team.
- The coaching you give to your team to help them grow, and the opportunities that your growing business provides to your team, will also help people feel motivated.
- Aligning with employees' personal core values will make motivation easier.
- Sharing your company's bigger picture with them will also help them get motivated and moving in the right direction.

In short, create a company where people want to work – because they're proud of it and they are rewarded for it and it aligns with their own personal targets – and your team will be highly motivated.

The most effective way to help people feel motivated is to figure out what inspires them, what their personal targets are, and show them how the particular project or task you're asking them to do will help them achieve their target. Does your employee desire to advance in the company? Show them how the challenging task that they are facing right now will help to hone their abilities for the future role they seek. Does your employee desire to earn enough money each week to provide for his family? Show him how important he is to the company and that showing up on time every day and working through to the end of the day will ensure his long-term employment with you so he can provide for his family for years to come.

Employee recognition is an important part of helping people feel motivated. If you reward employees when they do good work – work that gets you closer to your company's targets – you reinforce actions and behaviors that you want to see repeated.

Employee recognition is not just a way to show your employees that you're a nice guy; it is a way to encourage behavior that is advantageous to your company's success. In addition, employees who feel that their employers truly care about them and their wellbeing will produce better results. (Peer to peer recognition also helps – it's very powerful when one team member recognizes the contribution of another team member).

In fact, studies have shown that praise from a supervisor ranks higher than money, benefits, or incentives in conveying that a company values its employees. Recognizing an employee for work well done is also paramount to retaining that employee. Employee recognition has been shown to improve communication, productivity, and the workplace environment. Employees are more motivated to produce desirable outcomes, and their motivation influences their colleagues to do the same. Happier employees also tend to produce happier customers. Therefore, recognition of even a single action of a single employee can have far-reaching benefits.

An effective recognition system will be simple, immediate, and powerful. All employees should be eligible for recognition. When showing recognition, communicate it in such a way that everyone understands what specific actions are being recognized. You could communicate it through a company newsletter, an email announcement, at a staff meeting, or even through video. Never use a reward system in which upper management chooses the recipients. These systems end up being viewed as "favoritism" or they become ineffective because employees believe that "everybody will get their turn eventually".

Remember, most people get out of bed every day, fight traffic, and report to work because they need money. They don't necessarily like their jobs. That's why more money is not always a motivator for such people. Getting more money does not change anything; they still have to get out of bed every morning and go to work. So you need to find out what other factors will motivate your employees. How can you get them to perform better? From simple plaques to larger gifts and awards, there is a wide selection of awards for appreciating employees. Your award doesn't have to be expensive, nor does it have to have monetary value. It just needs to be important to the employee.

Additionally, the presentation of the award is, itself, a type of award because of the public recognition it provides. Create an event or awards ceremony, and have as many people as possible present. In certain instances, having the employee's family present can enhance the occasion and your purpose. Many people are proud to have their spouse or family know how important their work is and how they are appreciated. This can carry over and go a long way at home the next time they need to work late or make some other sacrifice for the company. People like to know their loved ones are in a good environment when they are away at work. They will be much more tolerant knowing how important and needed their loved one is on the job.

Take Action!

___ Stop doing actions (Actions you currently do now but should stop doing)

_____

_____

___ Keep doing actions (Actions you currently do now and should keep doing)

_____

_____

___ Start doing actions (Actions you don't do now but should start doing)

_____

_____

___ Who will do new actions? (Assign the action to yourself or someone else)

_____

_____

__ By when? (When will these actions be complete?)

_____

_____

POWER KEY #17: THE SECRET WAY TO SAVE MONEY AND MAKE MORE MONEY

Your employees are key to your business's success. Of course they are your representatives to customers and prospective customers, and many of the lessons in this book are about helping you to lead your team toward becoming better representatives of you. (And if you want even more strategies, I cover that in nearly every chapter of my book *The Secrets Of Business Mastery*).

Aside from being your company's representatives, they're also your eyes, ears, and boots on the ground, and this gives you a distinct advantage that can help you save money and make more money: Their work gives them an opportunity to discover ways to help you grow your business.

The unfortunate truth is that many business owners view their employees as a hassle – a group of reluctant workers who need to be wrangled and coerced. (Wake-up call: This exact belief becomes your reality. If you think your employees are a hassle, they are. But the opposite is true, too).

Your team, however, is a valuable asset and they all have a lot to bring to the table to help you dramatically grow your business in ways you didn't realize. All you need to do is to tap into their creativity.

For example, one employee might have a way to organize his truck that makes it more efficient to find tools when needed. Or another employee might think of a way to help your company save money on raw materials. Every employee is constantly out doing the work every day and they are naturally encountering opportunities for improvement (and often making some of those improvements themselves, proactively).

Chances are, there are creative solutions and ideas already happening at your business that you don't even realize. You should tap into that so that the ideas are shared among your team so that everyone benefits.

To do that, you'll want to build an atmosphere that encourages creativity. Many business owners might say "We already do that because we tell our employees that we're open to ideas" but that's not enough.

Simply stating that your business is open to ideas doesn't necessarily empower employees to share their ideas. In fact, employees are generally reluctant to make suggestions and express ideas because they fear appearing less intelligent and subjecting themselves to ridicule. You must create an environment of open expression through encouragement and restriction of judgment. Communication can only become truthful and beneficial through open listening.

One way to do this is by regularly asking your team questions to see what they're doing. For example, if you're walking around the shop area and you notice that an employee has a carefully organized truck, as him how he came up with that organization and listen to the thinking behind it. Then ask other employees how they organize their trucks and see how they each do. You'll only discover these opportunities for improvement when you ask employees.

Note: be sure to ask employees respectfully and with an open and enquiring mind. For example, asking the employee "why did you organize your truck like that?" might sound like you are judging how they organized their truck and then they might not give a good answer but rather a safe answer that will keep them from getting into trouble. But if you ask, "I noticed your truck is very organized and you seem to have a specific order that you keep everything in. I like how clean and neat it is. How did you choose this order and what do you like about it?" Notice the difference in how the question was asked?

Another way to tap into your employee's problem-solving creativity is to hold brainstorming sessions. Pick an area of the business that you want to work on and invite employees to the session to participate. Get creative and don't immediately judge peoples' answers. Listen to everything, accept all viewpoints, and then evaluate them later.

When you hold brainstorming sessions, be willing to invite many people in, even if the area that is being discussed doesn't directly impact them. True creativity comes from divergent thinking, and divergent thinking comes from other viewpoints (often the viewpoints that are very distinct from the topic being discussed).

Plan to hold brainstorming sessions regularly. Focus on areas that will save money, make money, or make an area of the business more efficient. And even consider giving financial prizes to the employees with the best ideas. Your team will surprise you and your business will benefit dramatically.

Your team is an invaluable asset to help grow your business and not just because they're out there serving customers. They have a much greater contribution to your business – both now and its ability to survive and thrive in the future.

Many times, leaders base an employee's performance on the job he is doing and how well the individual is producing within the boundaries of the job description, with no awareness of his potential. Leaders often shield themselves from insubordination and maintain control by creating and preserving the perception that they know everything. However, this persona stifles expression of ideas and knowledge and prevents the cultivation of inspiration and innovation among your workers. Keep it up and your employees will become discouraged and feel the job or company holds no potential for them.

Asking or demanding the best from your employees is pointless if you have no idea what their best is. Only by listening to their ideas will you encourage them to think and discover how great they might really be.

And, employees love sharing their ideas. Even if their ideas are not all implemented, employees feel that they are being listened to. And when ideas are implemented, employees feel a greater sense of ownership in the company.

Take Action!

___ Stop doing actions (Actions you currently do now but should stop doing)

_____

_____

___ Keep doing actions (Actions you currently do now and should keep doing)

_____

_____

___ Start doing actions (Actions you don't do now but should start doing)

_____

_____

___ Who will do new actions? (Assign the action to yourself or someone else)

_____

_____

___ By when? (When will these actions be complete?)

_____

_____

POWER KEY #18: LEADING OUTSOURCED COMPANIES & VENDORS

Very few companies will do all their own work "in-house." It's likely that some of the work will be outsourced to other professionals and businesses that specialize in that work.

There are many reasons to choose to outsource part of your business' activities. Here are a few:

- The cost for equipment is too high (example: outsourcing your printing work).
- You don't need the service to be completed regularly or during the same hours that your business operates; rather you need their services sporadically or as-needed (example: outsourcing your legal work).
- The service is not a core offering (example: outsourcing the cleaning of your company uniforms).
- In some cases, you may outsource part of your core offering that is too specialized to keep someone on full-time (example: you may run an electric company but you partner with a plumbing company who you bring in if you need to collaborate on a customer project). Or, you might outsource your core offering if you want to scale larger, faster.
- You might outsource something if you want to test a new service before you commit to it 100% (example: if you are a plumber and want to offer electrical service, you might outsource the electrical before committing 100% to adopting it as a tradeline).

Outsourcing should not be thought of as handing off a piece of your business to someone else so you don't have to think about it anymore. As with hiring a team, leading outsourcing still requires management skills. You still need to make sure they do the job you ask of them, and do it to your satisfaction. For example, if you outsource your legal work to an attorney, that shouldn't excuse you from paying attention to the progress of the work and seeking to understand what your attorneys are doing on your behalf. Your outsource team should be professional but consider them to be part of your team: a group that needs to be led.

Make your success important to your outsource partners by establishing good communication and rewarding them appropriately. I've built up such a relationship with my own outsource team that several companies I outsource to will meet regularly together to discuss how they can help my business (even without me being there).

Why do they do this? Because ultimately outsourcing is a partnership and we can help each other succeed when we each have the other partner's interest at heart.

Building A Positive Relationship With Your Team

Make sure your outsource partners share your vision. Obviously they will have their own vision (whether stated or unstated) but it should have similar concepts as yours. For example, if you desire to run the largest plumbing company in the state, it makes sense to hire an accounting firm that desires or has achieved statewide growth as well.

Negotiating outsourcing differs from employee pay negotiation. You can get quotes and compare services and products from companies. In most markets, there will be many companies to choose from – and even more services can be delivered online, which allows you to choose the best provider for you regardless of where they are located. Don't always choose the cheapest option. Instead, weigh the value they will deliver to your company and make sure that they are aligned with your core values and that they also have their own core values as well.

Make sure your specific requirements leave room for innovation. The complexity of outsourced services requires extra flexibility with risk/reward sharing that encourages optimal performance.

If you are outsourcing a portion of work that your employees feel they can do on their own, be aware that employee resistance can impact morale, productivity, and employee turnover, especially if they see their own job changing substantially. Discuss what is being outsourced and why. Assure employees of their job security and train them in their new roles.

Getting The Most From Your Outsource Team

Put clear performance measures in place. Specify your requirements in terms of outcomes. Create standards to measure performance. This will help ensure high quality service, when incentives and penalties are attached for over or under performance. These standards might need to evolve over time.

Setting clear communication channels is also essential. Make sure everyone knows how often you will be communicating and how to reach you. The more critical the outsource partner is to your business, the more often you'll need to communicate with them so schedule regular communications appropriately.

Establish a platform to manage your outsource vendors and ensure that everyone is on the same page. Sometimes this might be an occasional email but as your projects (and business) become bigger and more complex, you'll need a more robust platform to keep everyone moving in the same direction. This might be a simple forum tool (even a private Facebook group might work) or it might be a larger project management tool (such as Basecamp.com or Asana.com).

While you will still need to lead this outsource team by setting expectations and checking in regularly, you should also expect and encourage their own proactive effort as part of their delivery of service.

View your work with outsource partners as a collaboration: you bring your own ideas and vision of a particular project or task but you also rely on their expertise to complete the project or task.

Take Action!

__ Stop doing actions (Actions you currently do now but should stop doing)

_____

_____

__ Keep doing actions (Actions you currently do now and should keep doing)

_____

_____

__ Start doing actions (Actions you don't do now but should start doing)

_____

_____

__ Who will do new actions? (Assign the action to yourself or someone else)

_____

_____

__ By when? (When will these actions be complete?)

_____

_____

POWER KEY #19: HOLDING YOUR TEAM ACCOUNTABLE

In an ideal world, your team would all show up on time, do more than the work required, and leave work on time at the end of the day – all while completing their work ethically and according to your company guidelines.

Unfortunately, that doesn't always happen. We're human and some people choose to act in a way that runs counter to the ethical and operational standards you expect from your team. Although there are ways that you can keep this from happening a lot, you will always encounter this to some degree in your business.

Many of the strategies that I've described throughout this book will help to insulate your business from having this happen too often. When you hire superstars and empower them and motivate them and serve them, you'll keep more of the best teams.

But once in a while you'll still encounter an employee that needs to be held accountable for failing to act within your company's standards.

When that happens, employee discipline is necessary. While no business owner or manager loves to discipline employees, it's a key part of leadership and it's something that every business will need to face at one time or another.

But when should you discipline and how should you do it?

First, don't think of employee discipline as a last resort. See it as an opportunity to coach and correct on-the-go. It's just like disciplining your children: most parents coach, correct, and discipline their children in small ways throughout the day rather than waiting for the child to completely misbehave. Likewise with your team, employee discipline is a tool you can use regularly and positively to keep your team aligned. It is not something to be avoided, nor should it be thought of as the final measure before the employee is removed from the company. Broaden your thinking and think of employee accountability as something you do positively and constructively at all times.

Second, understand that not all discipline and accountability is equal. For example, showing up late should not have same consequence as stealing something. In my company, we have 3 rules: don't lie, cheat, or steal. Those are ethical boundaries that we simply won't tolerate and doing any of them results in instant removal from the company. But sometimes we need to discipline someone for something else that isn't an ethical issue but an operational one (i.e. showing up late or consistently refusing to complete a task in the way it needs to be done). In this case, we use a multi-step process (which I'll describe next) that gives the employee plenty of opportunity to correct their behavior.

Third, approach discipline as a multi-step coaching opportunity. When disciplinary action is necessary, here are the steps I use in my company when an employee's behavior needs to be corrected:

1. Verbalize the situation and put it in the employee's file.
2. If it happens again, document the situation and have them sign it.
3. If it happens a third time, the employee gets a week off, unpaid.
4. If it happens a fourth time, they are relocated out of the business.

Your employee handbook should be the guide for any discipline. Most employees will be aware if they have broken rules, and should have a clear understanding of the consequences.

Want to know the easiest way to discipline employees and hold them accountable? It all comes back to service: as a leader, you are there to serve your employees (and, of course, they are there to serve you and to serve your customers). You will get more out of them if you serve them. If an employee shows up late, don't jump on it as a discipline issue that needs to be reprimanded and immediately corrected.

Rather, approach it by asking yourself how you can serve the employee. Use this approach when talking to the employee. Perhaps you'll discover that the employee was late one time simply because they stopped to help at the scene of a car accident. Or perhaps you'll discover that the employee has been late twice in a week because their spouse is very ill and it requires extra work to get the kids to school in the morning. Or perhaps you'll discover that the employee has been late a few times in the month because they're not enjoying the team they are on.

These are three simple examples but they all have different solutions, and not necessarily ones that lead to a disciplinary reprimand. Can you think of a way that you can serve your employees in each scenario to create positive results in their lives and their work?

Thinking of these interactions as employee discipline will only get you worked up and get your employees worked up, and will not make your business an attractive environment to work in. But thinking of it positively as discipline and accountability ultimately to serve your employees will change how you approach the situation and allows you to create a positive culture.

All discipline should be done in private and handled on a case-by-case basis. Give the employee an opportunity to explain themselves.

Avoid the temptation to skip discipline because you want to be the nice guy or your employee's friend. By avoiding discipline when it's called for, you open the door for future problems – either from this employee who may repeat the same behavior because they didn't learn, or from other employees who feel that they were disciplined for the same problem. Treat everyone the same and discipline consistently.

The role of business owner and manager requires that you step up and discipline when it's called for. Accepting this as part of your duty helps to align your team to your business.

Take Action!

___ Stop doing actions (Actions you currently do now but should stop doing)

_____

_____

___ Keep doing actions (Actions you currently do now and should keep doing)

_____

_____

___ Start doing actions (Actions you don't do now but should start doing)

_____

_____

__ Who will do new actions? (Assign the action to yourself or someone else)

_____

_____

__ By when? (When will these actions be complete?)

_____

_____

POWER KEY #20: HOW TO REMOVE EMPLOYEES PROFESSIONALLY

As I've said earlier in this book, the work of a leader is hard. That's why not everyone can be a leader – they're just not willing to do the hard work.

One of the hardest parts of being a leader is when you identify someone on your team who should no longer be on your team.

After you have exhausted disciplinary measures or when an employee has committed an egregious act, you might be faced with having to remove that employee from the company.

In this chapter I'll show you how to remove that employee fairly, professionally, and responsibly, in a way that is best for you, for them, and for the company.

Just as in the last chapter, I would suggest that removing the employee is also a way to serve them. Yes, this probably sounds funny but it's true: The employee's actions have indicated that they are no longer interested or able to work at your company so you are serving them by helping them exit the company so they can find a future that is more aligned with their choices.

You should also note that not all employees who want to leave a company realize it right away. They shift (sometimes quickly; sometimes slowly) from being motivated to being unmotivated; from following your standards to not following your standards. So rather than quitting, an employee might just stop caring – not because they don't like working for you but because their own values or personal targets have shifted. So removing an employee isn't always a negative issue; it is serving them because you're helping them get take action to get realigned.

Removing the employee is serving them! And, it's also serving you, your business, the rest of your team, and your customers. Although you might not want to remove an employee from your team, avoiding the necessary work and keeping them on the team does not serve anybody!

Here's the most important thing to remember about removing employees: most of the time, you need to remove employees because of a failure to manage, coach, or train employees. Yes, there are occasionally other reasons to remove employees but most of the time it's because you as a leader did not adequately lead your employees and inspire them to give their very best at all times. Let this warning serve not as a reason to keep employees on even if they do a poor job but rather to create a culture in your business in which every employee is driven to do their very best and is inspired by you and empowered through training and coaching.

Now let's get into the details about how to remove an employee effectively.

Make sure you document everything on an ongoing basis through an employee's time with your company. That way, if a situation reaches the point where you have to remove an employee from you company, you have documentation to back up your decision. Collect the information together, including:

- The signed copy of the statement that says the employee read and fully comprehended the company employee handbook and the job description.
- The employee's scorecards and performance interview notes.
- A record of employee infractions documented with the date, time, and witnesses. Keep records on all of the employees' tasks, performances, infractions, and warnings. Make sure you have followed all policies and procedures in your employee handbook.
- Record how an employee's actions, behavior, or attitude has injured business and affected production, coworkers, and clients.

It's important to keep up this record on an ongoing basis to help you avoid accusations that you are removing the employee for some reason other than a failure to work at your company's standards.

The key to removing an employee effectively is to be prepared and then to complete the task without delay. Many business owners view it as an unpleasant task and so they delay and procrastinate on the necessary activities. However, preparation can help you navigate this complex and emotionally-charged situation effectively. Here's how you can prepare:

- Anticipate the need to replace the employee.
- Prepare a checklist and timetable for the day.
- Assure confidentiality. Regardless of the reason for termination, be respectful.
- Find privacy. Keep a door open but not where others will hear. Be sure to have a witness.
- Have back pay and personal belongings ready.
- Notify security, if necessary and available. Ensure a safe departure from the building.
- Make sure all proprietary information has been confiscated, future access prevented, and passwords changed.

Never give an employee notice that they that they are going to be terminated. This will help to protect you from further problems, theft, or damage to company property as a result of retribution. If you feel an ethical obligation, pay them the equivalent of time of notice.

Do an exit interview with the employee to see what each of you has learned. Although the situation may be emotionally charged for both of you, work through a prepared set of questions and record all feedback. The employee will still be able to provide you with useful information that you can learn from.

The time limit for bringing an unfair dismissal claim is three months from the dismissal date, but this can be extended where it is not reasonably practicable.

Fortunately, if you apply many of the powerful keys I've described throughout this book, you will dramatically reduce the number of employee removals you will need to make: by hiring superstars, you'll hire people who want to work at the level your company expects; by motivating employees and creating opportunities for them in a culture that values them, you'll keep more employees around; by serving your employees, you'll have to address any issues that may cause them to want to leave.

Take Action!

___ Stop doing actions (Actions you currently do now but should stop doing)

_____

_____

___ Keep doing actions (Actions you currently do now and should keep doing)

_____

_____

___ Start doing actions (Actions you don't do now but should start doing)

_____

_____

___ Who will do new actions? (Assign the action to yourself or someone else)

_____

_____

___ By when? (When will these actions be complete?)

_____

_____

POWER KEY #21: PEOPLE LEADERSHIP SUCCESS STORIES

Years ago, after burning out, my business partner Rob came to me and said he wanted to leave the company. My choices seemed to be: to continue without him (and burn out myself) or shut the company down. Then I realized that we had a third choice – we could make a change and build a business that we wanted to build.

So we went out and studied other businesses – even businesses in other industries, like Disney, Zappos, Amazon and more. We weren't looking for best practices of the service industry, we were looking for best practices… period.

Today, we're over $23 million (and growing) with over 100 trucks on the road and over 140 employees. I'm proud to say that we've become a success story.

As a service business owner, you may look to my company to give you some of the best practices for your business. And, you might also do what Rob and I did when we started turning our company around – look to other companies in other industries that are doing well. According to CNNMoney.com, the ten most admired companies in the area of people leadership are as follows:

1. FedEx
2. Procter & Gamble
3. Google
4. General Electric
5. Genentech
6. Starbucks
7. CHS
8. Kinder Morgan
9. Kinder Morgan Energy Partners
10. Exxon Mobil

Let's take a look at the philosophies of some of these organizations when it comes to the human resources aspect of their business.

Starting with number one, the FedEx website contains the following statement about its people: "To provide the level of service and quality necessary to become, and to remain, the leader in the air express cargo transportation industry, Federal Express has developed a unique

91

relationship with its employees, based on a people-first corporate philosophy. Founder and CEO Frederick Smith determined to make employees an integral part of the decision-making process, due to his belief that 'when people are placed first they will provide the highest possible service, and profits will follow'."

Similarly, Procter & Gamble makes the following statement in an advertisement recruiting employees to the organization: "Procter and Gamble is #1 in People Management. We are committed to building and developing our organization through our 'Promote from Within' philosophy. We primarily recruit talented people at entry level with the intention of having a productive long-term relationship that develops them to take on future leadership roles."

Putting people first seems to be the bedrock of these two successful companies' philosophies.

Shouldn't people leadership be just as important in your organization? Companies that put people leadership in the forefront, such as the two mentioned above, and the one discussed below, seem not only to succeed in that area, but also are overall successes. All three of these companies are among CNNMoney.com's top twenty most admired businesses overall.

Fortune Online states the following regarding Starbucks: "It's green, it's human, it's politically correct, it sells a popular product and provides a comfy place to hang out and consume same – what's not to like?"

Howard Schultz was manager of U.S. operations for Hammarplast, a Swedish firm that manufactured drip coffeemakers, when he convinced the owners of Starbucks to hire him as Director of Marketing and Operations in 1982. The owners resisted his plan to actually brew and serve their coffee in retail stores and Schultz quit. He started his own coffee-bar business and bought Starbucks for $3.8 million one year later. His desire was "to build a company with soul." His people leadership policies, such as providing all employees working at least twenty hours per week with comprehensive health coverage and offering an employee stock option plan, resulted in loyalty and low turnover. He offers four principles to those who wish to follow in his footsteps (source: myprimetime.com/work/ge/schultzbio):

1. Do not be threatened by people smarter than you. Companies grow when the owners hire people smarter than themselves.
2. Compromise anything but your core values.
3. Seek to renew yourself even when you are hitting home runs.
4. Everything matters.

While you might not aspire to own a company like FedEx, Procter & Gamble, or Starbucks, the lessons learned from these success stories can help you to run your business more effectively.

As a business owner, you should always be coaching your team to improve… but just because you are a business owner doesn't meant that improvement has stopped for you! There are many ways you can improve – from reading books and watching online videos (such as my ServiceKey TV videos, which are recorded specifically for the service industry) to attending workshops and seminars… from listening to podcasts (like my Secrets Of Business Mastery podcast) to hiring a coach, mentor, or business transformer who can give you one-on-one guidance.

Take Action!

___ Stop doing actions (Actions you currently do now but should stop doing)

_____

_____

___ Keep doing actions (Actions you currently do now and should keep doing)

_____

_____

___ Start doing actions (Actions you don't do now but should start doing)

_____

_____

__ Who will do new actions? (Assign the action to yourself or someone else)

_____

_____

__ By when? (When will these actions be complete?)

_____

_____

POWER KEY #22: HOW TO GET ALONG WITH YOUR TEAM LIKE THE BRADY BUNCH

Your employees are a diverse group of people who come together for the workday and collaborate to work for you, serve your customers, and earn their salary. Although their target is the same, and the work they are required to do is the same, each one of your employees is unique. This uniqueness has the potential to create conflict in the workplace, and although some *constructive* conflict is healthy, too much conflict and disagreement will hurt your ability to serve customers and put your business at risk.

Establish parameters in your business about how your employees can get along with each other. Although you can't force a friendship, you can create a respectful, collaborative workplace where people may not always agree but they can work together for the common good. Share the following advice with your employees to help them get along with each other:

1. **Live the core values**: The company's core values express what the company stands for. Make sure your actions are aligned with the stated core values.
2. **Watch how you respond:** How you say something is as important, or more so, than what you say. How many times have you been criticized by someone and felt angry because of his tone of voice or attitude? Not responding or walking away when you feel resentment or anger will deflate the situation.
3. **Use promises sparingly**: People seem to remember a broken promise forever, even as something as simple as offering to pick up their lunch while you are out, and not doing it. People will consider you irresponsible and you'll get a bad reputation when you don't do what you say you will.
4. **Listen to others**: You can gain the confidence of people by being a good listener. Learn to listen without passing judgment. While this might be sometimes difficult, you will keep the lines of communication open and build trust with people who know they can talk to you about anything. Listening to people makes them feel important and worthy. When you practice listening with empathy and without judgment, those people will be there for you

should you ever need them. Here's a good rule of thumb: Listen for five minutes before responding for one minute.

5. **Win every argument**: The only way to win any argument is to avoid it. Don't let yourself get into arguments with others. Learn to discuss subjects without opposing viewpoints. You can always agree to disagree with anyone. (Note: don't confuse arguments with conflict. Conflict is healthy, arguments are not).

6. **Leave your trash at home**: Don't talk about personal issues in the workplace. When you walk in the door, leave your personal life outside.

7. **Never talk about anyone who is not present**: Refuse to gossip or speculate about other people. Gossip is a harmful and vicious snake that will most often turn and bite you.

8. **Be considerate**: Do not laugh at the expense of others. Be considerate and think about their feelings.

9. **Ignore what others say about you**: You will appear strong when you do not react to what others say about you. Let your actions speak for you.

10. **Keep your work ethic in check**: Do your best and set an example for others. Find the pride and passion in your work.

11. **Encourage others – give them a good reputation to live up to**: Compliment others on their work and progress. Always have something good to say about people.

12. **Be optimistic**: An optimistic person attracts people. Keep your attitude in check and look for the good in everything.

13. **Be independent**: Stick to your guns and don't be swayed when people resort to gossip or a lower standard of behavior.

14. **Return borrowed items**: If you borrow something, return it as soon as you are finished.

15. **Try the source first**: Before going over someone's head with a simple issue, try approaching them first. If you cannot work it out, then seek the assistance of your supervisor.

16. **Focus on your work**: Don't concern yourself with your coworkers' productivity unless their job is directly affecting yours.

17. **Remember you're not the boss**: Don't try to take charge of others when it's not your right or responsibility.

18. **Don't discuss pay**: Pay is a very personal matter and varies among employees depending on their experience and position. It is best to keep it to yourself to avoid jealousy or competition.

19. **Don't do personal chores on company time**: This will create animosity among your coworkers.

20. **Your reputation is everything**: You can build it and control it yourself or you can allow it to be built by default (outside of your control). Doesn't it make more sense to build it and control it?

Take Action!

__ Stop doing actions (Actions you currently do now but should stop doing)

_____

_____

__ Keep doing actions (Actions you currently do now and should keep doing)

_____

_____

__ Start doing actions (Actions you don't do now but should start doing)

_____

_____

__ Who will do new actions? (Assign the action to yourself or someone else)

_____

_____

__ By when? (When will these actions be complete?)

_____

_____

NEXT STEPS

In this short action-focused book, you've learned 22 powerful keys to help you transform your team, master your leadership, and lead with vision. The tools in this book can help you to step up from being the boss to being an inspiring leader with employees who want to follow you. Use this as a guide to help align your team and to teach you how to grow as a leader.

These steps are only the beginning. Use these tools daily in your business. Here are other steps you should do as well:

1. Bookmark CEOwarrior.com, read the blog, watch the videos, sign up for the weekly newsletter, and learn more about the events and the Warrior Circle.
2. Get my books from Amazon:
    a. *The Secrets of Business Mastery* for the 12 areas of mastery that can transform your business in 90 days or less.
    b. *Secrets of Communication Mastery* for 18 powerful keys to help you communicate more effectively with your team, your customers, and anyone else.
3. Get the audio CD of The Secrets of Business Mastery at CEOwarrior.com/sobmaudiocd.
4. Watch for an upcoming Warrior Fast Track Academy where you'll spend 4 days working through many powerful strategies to build exciting, profitable change in your business. Visit CEOwarrior.com/events for more information.
5. Bookmark my magazine for the home service industry, HomeServiceMaxMag.com, and read each issue cover-to-cover, making notes and implementing changes as you go. (And, be sure to like the Facebook page at Facebook.com/HomeServiceMaxMag).
6. Bookmark my podcast, CEOwarrior.com/podcastshow, and watch for each new episode to reveal powerful strategies to grow your home service business.
7. Visit CEOwarrior.com to connect with me on Facebook, Twitter, LinkedIn, YouTube, and other social media.

Service business owners: Are you running your business? Or are you running on empty?

Many service business owners are shocked to discover that running a service business can be an exhausting, expensive struggle. But it doesn't have to be. You don't have to sacrifice your money, your health, and your time with family.

In *The Secrets of Business Mastery*, Business Ninja Mike Agugliaro reveals how you can take charge of your business, dominate your market, and achieve the kind of dramatic results that you've only dreamed of. You'll discover powerful secrets like:

- Mike's transformational approach to service (this is a game-changer) and how it brings in a flood of higher-paying customers.
- The exact step-by-step market domination strategies (and Mike's proprietary checklist) to massively increase the effectiveness of every marketing campaign.
- A surprising new way to approach your finances to make more money and put more profit in your pocket.
- His time-saving way to find the best employees, and the technologies he uses to empower his team.
- Plus hundreds of other proven strategies and actions to implement into your business immediately.

Mike will reveal his $30+ million dollar (and growing) blueprint to transform your business and achieve wealth and freedom. He'll lay out, step-by-step, exactly what you need to do daily in 12 areas of your business to take it to the next level.

Learn more at CEOwarrior.com/masterybook

Listen to the CEO Warrior Podcast

Whether you're at your desk, in your car, or out for a walk, Mike Agugliaro's CEO Warrior Podcast is the perfect companion.

Each week, Mike shares his best strategies with you on topics like leadership, business start-up, how to grow your business, how to stop over-paying your taxes, and many more topics that are immediately impactful to your service business. You'll also hear Mike interview A-list guests who share their insight as well.

If you've never heard Mike before, this is a great way to get a glimpse into how he thinks – you'll hear his signature "no-holds-barred" style as he shares proven raw and real strategies that he perfected in-the-trenches.

And if you're familiar with Mike, this is another great way to hear from him and apply his game-changing strategies in your business.

Every show is packed full of practical information and motivation for every service business owner. Subscribe to them, listen to them over and over – they're the perfect way to stay informed and motivated no matter where you are.

Download free episodes on iTunes and at
https://ceowarrior.com/podcastshow
.

Are you tired of treading water – staying busy in your business but never really getting ahead? Are you ready to discover the most powerful strategies to create real change, growth, and market domination in your business?

Whether you're new and totally overwhelmed or you're a seasoned pro and looking to reignite, The Warrior Fast Track Academy can show you how to get to the next level.

Warrior Fast Track Academy is my 4-day hands-on event where I guide you and a group of like-minded service business owners through the exact plan that I used to build a $30+ million (and growing) business. I'll reveal the blueprint and how you can implement the same blueprint into **your** business, with all areas of mastery planned out and ready to be plugged in. You'll be motivated and inspired to lead positive, profitable change in your company and take your business to never-before-seen heights.

Business owners who have attended the Warrior Fast Track Academy have said it's "life changing" and gone on to build successful businesses all around the world.

If you want to take control of your business and your future, Warrior Fast Track Academy is THE event to make that happen. To see what others are saying about Warrior Fast Track Academy, and to pre-register for an upcoming event, go to CEOwarrior.com/events

Have you ever wished you had a "Warrior Family" that could simultaneously hold you accountable for growing beyond your best self – and at the same time support your quest to get there?

Congratulations, you're home! If you elect to join Warrior Circle, this is what we do.

During the upcoming year, we will revolutionize your business and your life together. The Warrior Circle is committed to simplicity and balance. Together, we'll blow your wealth, freedom and personal goals out of the water by focusing on massive business building and life strategies.

We will also support you as you incorporate the 5 Dimensions of Life and Business Mastery – **Belief, Relationships, Health, Wealth, and Freedom** – and help you design activities and surroundings to support an amazing life!

This program is designed for go-getters and people who are ready to make the commitment and take action to boost their business.

To learn more about the Warrior Circle, and to see if you qualify to participate in the Mastermind, get in touch at CEOwarrior.com/contact

Read The Free Magazine Written For The Home Service Industry

Discover new information, insight, and industry-specific success stories in **Home ServiceMAX** – the free online magazine written for home service business owners.

Each issue of Home ServiceMAX is packed with practical tips and strategies that you can implement right away into your home service business. They're field-tested and written by experts and industry insiders.

Home ServiceMAX will help you improve your sales, marketing, finance, human resources and customer service. Keep it on hand as you develop best practices to meet your team's unique challenges.

Whether you're a plumber, electrician, carpenter, roofer, builder, painter or specialist in any other service industry trade, to survive you must also stand out as a business leader. We designed this magazine to help you achieve that goal.

Each easy-to-read issue is available online for free. Check out the articles and make sure you have a pen and paper in hand to write down all the actions you'll want to take when you're done each article.

Read the current issue and subscribe here: **HomeServiceMaxMag.com** .

ABOUT THE AUTHOR
MIKE AGUGLIARO, BUSINESS WARRIOR

 As Seen On

Mike Agugliaro helps his clients grow their service businesses utilizing his $30+ Million Warrior Fast Track Academy Blueprint, which teaches them how to achieve massive wealth and market domination.

Two decades ago, he founded Gold Medal Electric with his business partner Rob. After nearly burning out, he and Rob made a change: they developed a powerful blueprint that grew the company. Today, Gold Medal Service is now the top service industry provider in Central New Jersey. With over 140 staff and 100 trucks on the road, Gold Medal Service now earns over $30+ million in revenue each year.

Mike is a transformer who helps service business owners and other entrepreneurs master themselves and their businesses, take control of their dreams and choices, and accelerate their life and business growth to new heights. Mike is the author of the popular book *The Secrets Of Business Mastery*, in which he reveals 12 areas that all service business owners need to master.

Mike speaks and transforms around the world; his Warrior Fast Track Academy events are popular, transformational events for service business owners; he also leads a mastermind of business owners known as Warrior Circle. Mike has been featured in MSNBC, Financial Times, MoneyShow, CEO World, and more.

Mike is an avid martial artist who has studied karate, weaponry, jujitsu, and has even developed his own martial art and teaches it to others. The discipline of martial arts equips him to see and act on opportunities, create change in himself and others, and see that change through to successful completion.

Mike is a licensed electrician and electrical inspector, he is a certified Master Fire Walk Instructor, certified professional speaker, and a licensed practitioner of Neuro-Linguistic Programming (NLP).

Whether firewalking, breaking arrows on his neck, studying martial arts, transforming businesses, or running his own business, Mike Agugliaro leads by powerful example and is changing the lives and businesses of service business owners everywhere.

Mike lives in New Jersey with his wife and two children.

CONNECT WITH MIKE AGUGLIARO

Connect with Mike in the following places and find even more free resources and strategies to help you grow your business.

Website: **CEOWARRIOR.com** – Go here now to get free resources, including chapters from Mike's book and a library of resources.

Warrior App: **CEOWARRIOR.com/warriorapp** – stay up-to-date on the latest strategies and events by downloading the Warrior App for iOS and Android.

Podcast: **CEOWARRIOR.com/podcast**

Events: **CEOWARRIOR.com/events**

Social: Visit **CEOWARRIOR.com** to connect with Mike on Facebook, Twitter, LinkedIn, and elsewhere.

Home ServiceMAX Magazine: **HomeServiceMaxMag.com**

Made in the USA
Middletown, DE
14 August 2017